POETRY IDOL

TREASURED RHYMES

EDITED BY
ALLIE JONES

First published in Great Britain in 2019 by:

Young Writers
Est. 1991

Young Writers
Remus House
Coltsfoot Drive
Peterborough
PE2 9BF
Telephone: 01733 890066
Website: www.youngwriters.co.uk

All Rights Reserved
Book Design by Camilla Vidot
© Copyright Contributors 2019
Softback ISBN 978-1-83928-523-3

Printed and bound in the UK by BookPrintingUK
Website: www.bookprintinguk.com
YB0425F

Foreword

Our latest competition, Poetry Idol, focuses on the people that these young poets look up to. Using a mix of imagination, expression and poetic styles, this anthology is an impressive snapshot of the inventive, original and skilful writing of young people today, expressing their appreciation for the people, and things, that mean the most to them.

Young Writers was established in 1991 to nurture creativity in our children and young adults, to give them an interest in poetry and an outlet to express themselves. Seeing their work in print will encourage them to keep writing as they grow and become our poets of tomorrow.

Selecting the poems has been challenging and immensely rewarding. The effort and imagination invested by these young writers makes their poems a pleasure to enjoy reading time and time again.

CONTENTS

Independent Entries

Krystal-Louise Down (7)	1
Favour Joy Olorunfemi	2
Mahanoor Zaman (11)	4
Liam Kanyepi (16)	6
Gurpreet Kaur Singh (12)	8
Stephen Altay (10)	10
Aaryan Thomas-Michael Manarkattu (10)	12
Adrien Rider	14
Eva Rothlisberger (8)	16
Macy Hall (18)	18
Gabriel Haroon (7)	20
Maria Abid (12)	22
Rebecca Obasuyi (13)	24
Jade Athwal-McNair (18)	26
Oluwatimilehin Deborah Kehinde (10)	28
Satiya Bekelcha Yaya	30
Ellie Webster (13)	32
Lola Gosling (13)	33
Lucy Higgins	34
Raniya Nazam Khan (8)	36
Sareena Padayachy (11)	37
Mariyam Tehseen (12)	38
Mehmuna Kausar	40
Bethan Worrall (11)	42
Areeb Tahira	44
Rishika Raghunandanan	46
Fiona Jones (11)	48
Adam Faldeen Wareshallee (14)	49
Eunice Opemipo Olagbolabo (10)	50
Michael C Hansell (17)	52
Xander Luca (7)	54
Vishnupriya Ramamurthy	55
Sophiyah Hannah Torabally (12)	56
Aysha Afridi (11)	58
Abigail Lewis (12)	59
Ysabella Jo Strudwick (14)	60
Kathryn Blades (11)	62
Margot Grand (10)	63
Asia Shaddad (19)	64
Gurleen Gupta	65
Noemi Kufera (9)	66
Joseph Lawrence (9)	68
Imethma Weerarathna	70
Denny Kurera (14)	71
Rezwan Islam (11)	72
Sneha Daga (13)	73
Nicole Zheng	74
Rohun Manarkattu	75
Simisola Nancey Majekodunmi (12)	76
Beth Anderson (15)	78
Habiba Begum	79
Madeleine Francesca Lake	80
Olivia Lambert (10)	81
Grace Eighteen (9)	82
Claire Lucy Gee (18)	83
Colby Lewis Blackborow	84
Shania Miah	85
Deborah Esan	86
Tanisha Zaman (12)	87
Katie Adeosun (12)	88
Alicia Geere (11)	89
Ella-Mai McKitten (8)	90
Eisha Miah (11)	91
Lucyanne Reid	92
Sharmili Fatema (10)	93
Femy Biju (10)	94

Name	#	Name	#
Leah Weston (13)	96	Teghvir Singh (11)	139
Grace Kirkham (10)	97	Ruby Zelouf (6)	140
Rabia Islam Chowdhury	98	Lily Morris (10)	141
Noor-Ul-Ain Bhatti (15)	99	Lily Doherty	142
Elham Alizadah	100	Nicole Abitimo (7)	143
Jameela Mansour (13)	101	Megha Basu	144
Leah Mae Wilkes (12)	102	Elsie May Lightfoot (8)	145
Amelia May Lacey (8)	103	Elise-May Jee (15)	146
Tyler Jessop (15)	104	Ellyce Robinson	147
Trey Devonte Mclean (16)	105	Sasha Shadbolt (10)	148
Georgina Neillings (9)	106	Hannah Fallon	149
Charlie Caine (7)	107	Maymuna Alma Ejaz Ahmed (9)	150
Lucy Arnold (11)	108	Tayyibah Begum (10)	151
Olivia Morrell (15)	109	Jessica Dickens (10)	152
Evie O'Meara (11)	110	Ishma Ahmed (5)	153
Karolina Mrozinska (8)	111	Ayomide Deborah Aboyeji (10)	154
Joanna Majchrzyk (13)	112	Imaan Siddique (12)	155
Amelia-Jane Charleton (8)	113	Isabelle Alice Williams	156
Khadija Ajmal (13)	114	Lucy Hollis (16)	157
Alesha Akhtar (11)	115	Jayden Fahy (6)	158
Holly Ferns	116	Tess Diane Black (8)	159
Hakeem Hafidz	117	Dhruv Bhudia (7)	160
Aditi Bilawar (9)	118	Keeley Marie Seren Edwards	161
Mohamed Awadalkarim (11)	119	Nadia Aber Okwera (10)	162
Atheesh Ramesh (14)	120	Ruby Putnam (10)	163
Grace Upshall	121	Johanna Goron (8)	164
Cece Anang	122	Emaan Basharat (10)	165
Jasper Collins (10)	123	Libby Burbanks (9)	166
Poppy Tester	124	Afoma Anita Onwuokwu (10)	167
Gia Oubhie (5)	125	Megan Angharad Lois Pritchard (16)	168
Lily McElroy (10)	126		
Evelyn Louise Brandt (8)	127	Jasmin Pulkova	169
Ava Dobie (9)	128	Teddy Hawkins (6)	170
Momina Khan	129	Maryam Khanom (8)	171
Molly Charlton (9)	130	Noah Thomas Howard (5)	172
Israt Orpa Ahmed (13)	131	Maisy-Lou Tredinnick	173
Emily McGhee (14)	132	Sofia-Anne Cardall (6)	174
Shona Pandey (10)	133	Freya Addison McKean (9)	175
Jessica Beck	134	Maya Devaskar (7)	176
Sophia Hussain	135		
Chiara Gavazzi (9)	136		
Carla Maitena Burns (9)	137		
Lola Terry-Corneille (13)	138		

Cheltenham College, Cheltenham

Clara Nelson (6) 177

Cooks Spinney Primary Academy & Nursery, Cooks Spinney

Sapphire Balding (8) 178
Gabriel Elms (8) 179

Gorringe Park Primary School, Mitcham

Jachin Idehen-Nathaniel 180

Hazel Slade Primary Academy, Hazel Slade

Lauryn Grace Wilkes (10) 181
Daniel Tonks (10) 182
Ezra Nathaniel Davies (9) 183
Noah Boden (9) 184

Kenmore Park Junior School, Kenton

Abdia Mohamed Irshad (8) 185

Lyford Cay International School, Bahamas

Melissa Beukes (9) 186
Alexia Zatarain (9) 188

Marshfields School, Dogsthorpe

Jakey Brannigan 190
James O'Doherty (14) 191

NCEA Duke's Secondary School, Ashington

Emma Louise Ross (14) 192

Oxford Sixth Form College, Oxford

.... 193
Luke Kim (17) 194

Rosstulla School, Newtownabbey

Hannah Potsworth (14) 195
Ben Crawford (13) 196
Lewis Donnelly (12) 197

Southchurch High School, Southend-on-Sea

Finnley Higgins (11) 198
Jacob Thomas Gawley (12) 199
Gaius Ware (12) 200
Arrianne Lea (12) 201
Jaimie Parks (12) 202
Ana-Albina Vreme (12) 203
Madeline Atkin (12) 204
Khadija Nobre Dos Santos Costa (12) 205
Chloe Downs (11) 206
Molly Phillips (12) 207
Alfie Hunt (12) 208
Jessica Poole (12) 209
Emily Potts (12) 210
Joe Davies (12) 211
Alex Taylor (12) 212
Thomas Morgan Hucker (12) 213
Will Turner (11) 214
Alfie Peck (12) 215
Erica Bristow (12) 216
Dylan Jewell (12) 217
Bobby Reynolds (12) 218

Wouldham All Saints CE Primary School, Wouldham

Alexander Guérin-Hassett (9) 219

THE POEMS

My Idol

My idol is my auntie, she's very kind and sweet,
She's generally fantastic, the nicest person you could meet,
She is smiley and bubbly, she cares 'bout me too,
She's my auntie Emma and I'm her Krissie-Lou,
She's pretty and she's clever, she's honest and she's smart,
She'll do anything for anyone with the purest of her heart
Because she's my auntie Emma and I'm her Krissie-Lou,
She's friends with loads of people, works hard at the same time,
But always has time to pop and see me at mine
She's my auntie Emma and I'm her Krissie-Lou
Emma is my idol and one day I would like to be like her too.
There isn't anyone quite like her, she's amazing in so many ways.
I look forward to our special quality time days,
I am only seven and she is 21
But she is guiding me now to what I will become
I look up to Emma, she is so special to me
The best of it is, she doesn't see what I see,
How amazing she is whilst watching me grow
But one day she will see I learnt all she knows
Because she's my auntie Emma and I'm her Krissie-Lou,
We'll be best friends forever, that I know is true.

Krystal-Louise Down (7)

Love Myself, Love Yourself

You can call them artists, you can call them idols,
Any other title won't bother their freedom.
They're proud of it, so free of it,
No more irony, they've always just been them.

BTS are my idols, a South Korean boy group.
They've taken over the world with songs like 'Chicken Noodle Soup',
Not even they expected all of this success,
But their hard work paid off, while now, they can sit and rest.

"Kill them with success, bury them with a smile!"
It's what Kim Namjoon said, but won't that take a while?
They have everything they want, everything they need,
Yet they still stay humble, like they're still growing seeds.

The members are RM, Suga, J-Hope,
The rappers of the group,
RM and Suga, true geniuses,
J-Hope, bright all the way through.

Jin, Jimin, V and Jungkook,
The truly talented singers.
Surprisingly, they aren't that bad,
But they play just like toddlers.

They make me smile on my saddest days,
They wash all of my pain away.
Their music I might not understand,
But I know it's a huge helping hand.

It's fascinating just how seven people can make you see,
The true beauty of yourself, the harsh reality,
They helped me,
So many people realise the importance of mental health,
This is what they taught me:
'Love myself, love yourself'.

Mahanoor Zaman (11)

They Did It For Me

(This poem is about my admiration for my parents and understanding the perilous and courageous journey they took to get me where I am today, being thankful that my parents had the courage to stick with me even when I was at the lowest points in my life.)

They did it for me.
We and a pearl entered a tunnel filled with darkness and the concealed,
Endless bellowing; cries awaited,
Overwhelmed with the fear of not knowing our next steps,
Comprehending that a misstep could cause this precious pearl to be ravaged,
Almost causing us to forget how to walk.
We came equipped with nothing but a toy and a bottle of milk.

They did it for me.
Day in, day out,
We'd wondered what treasures our prime pearl would possess,
That it would shine its brightest and nothing less.

They did it for me.
We picked this pearl up off the dirty tunnel floor when it was down,
Praying that when we had reached that light,
We'd know if it glistened vividly after being embodied by the darkness,

Never knowing if we'd see the light.
They endured this for me.
Anyone with a smile on their face after going through great affliction,
Is an automatic inspiration like when you automatically,
Look away from a bright light.

They did it for me.
We lost hours of sleep in that tunnel of darkness,
Cries invaded the peace like time changed my baby into a teenager.

So Mum, Dad, why did you go all that way just to reach the light at the end of that tunnel?

We did it for you.

Liam Kanyepi (16)

That's My...?

Oh my dear mother!
My dear mum!
Oh my dear mummy!
My dear mom!
There are so many words to describe you:
Sympathetic,
Caring,
Loving.
"How can one person be so many things?" someone asks
"That's my mother!" every daughter, son, child replies.

You are the sun and I orbit around you.
You are my best friend and I share every secret too.
You are always there for me when I need you.
Again the question is asked...
"How can someone be so many things?"
I and every other child replies, "That's my mum!"

I may not always show it,
But I love you dearly
I am grateful for how you always listen and speak to me sincerely.
How you faced an immense amount of pain,
Just to make sure I was born.
I am so thankful,
So thankful that no words can express it... but I hope this poem will.

"How can someone be this close to you?" a stranger asks in confusion.
"That's my mummy," children reply in unity.

You may be my best friend...
But that doesn't stop you from being my idol.
You are my past, present and future.
Your kind nature is the reason I look up to you!
You show me the light in every path!
In me you always have faith!
"How is this possible?"
"That's my mom."
Believe it or not.

Gurpreet Kaur Singh (12)

My Best Friend, Honey The Golden Labrador

Honey is my Golden Labrador and she is my best friend
She never leaves my side and we will be friends to the end

Whenever I feel sad, she will come and lick my face
And I will throw her ball for her because she loves to chase

Every day she waits for me to come home from school
And then jumps up and licks my face, covering me in her drool

She isn't allowed upstairs, but can be very sneaky
Until I say, "Where's Honey?" and then hear the stairs all creaky

She loves lying in the garden, shading under the willow tree
Cocking her head to one side, so curious watching the honeybee

When people walk past her she runs over, her tail wagging to say 'Hi'
Everyone that meets her loves her so much they hate saying goodbye

When we go up the hills, my mum sets her free
She runs and jumps in the river, her face full of glee

She is eight years old now, that's 56 in dog years
Knowing she won't be here forever brings out all my fears

I love my dog so very much, her big, brown, chocolate button eyes
And when we leave her home alone I hate to hear her whimper cries

She truly is an amazing dog and best friend of mine
I am so thankful she is a part of my life because she really makes me shine.

Stephen Altay (10)

My Idol

Well, let me think about that,
If I want to succeed, who do I look at?
It sounds as easy as one, two, three,
But it's not just one person, not for me!

What is an idol, someone I want to be?
Who I've been looking at since the age of three?
I can't remember anyone specific,
No one seems outstandingly terrific.

So it'll have to be a combination,
But who'll be included and in what formation?
I look up to my mum, as with my dad,
But who else will I need to add?

The mixture is growing, but I'm looking for more,
Who do I look at more than I've ever before?

My grandad's an important figure in my life,
He lived in a world of endless strife.
He faced his problems with a bold heart,
And now he's created works of art.

That's not all, I have two uncles who are smart,
And my other grandad's as sharp as a dart.
I love my late grandma so much, though I never, ever met her.
But there's one thing I know for sure: the other one sings better!

Of course, I come back with a great conclusion,
I look up to everyone that I put in this fusion!
So that's basically all, that would be everyone I know,
Because they each have something that could help me grow!

Aaryan Thomas-Michael Manarkattu (10)

In Cat's Claw (My Poetry Idol)

Like words in fire and in cat's claw
The stained pages of ink, mean so much more
A journey, though eyes that are not your own
Through stories of those, you're never alone
First one book, which I dared read
From an enclosed cage, my mind was freed

Just a simple cat, fur of fire
To live in the wild, did he aspire
Just one paw step, to follow your dream
And soon he did rule, the wild in his bloodstream

Kin of his enemy, left far away
On a dangerous journey, he dared did stray
A cat from each world, soon closer than clan
A new home's in sight, the journey began

Three kits were born, from blood of the flame
Power from the stars, a prophecy to gain
A secret revealed, cuts deep like a claw
The three was now two, their secret no more

A new silver kit, was born to her fate
The darkness was rising, no time to hesitate

Betrayal from within, evil encroaching
Four minds became one, old ways out of motion

Your path was lit by the glowing half moon
Find what's in the dark, was what you must do
The exile was over, the sky was now light
All five clans together, the future looked bright

Of phoenix's wing I dared to take flight
A vision of stars, light my dreams tonight
Towering pages upon pages of salvation
For more to withhold, a sweet desperation
A soul that is fixed, once was asunder
I thank you for my hope, Erin Hunter.

Adrien Rider

Rosa Parks!

I only sat at the front of the bus,
What's wrong with that?
I sat with white instead of black,
What's wrong with that?
I stood up for my colour of skin,
What's wrong with that?
I didn't want to sit at the back, with black,
What's wrong with that?
Sitting at the back is insanity,
So I fearlessly went and did something different,
Guess what?
I sat at the front instead of the back,
Of course, with black.
Everyone was racist back then,
You would be judged by your skin,
Insane!
I knew the bus driver, James Blake,
He told me to enter at the back,
Of course, with black,
But I refused.
"Don't go at the back, too racist,"
I kept on muttering.
When I was little,
I went to school,
Of course, with black,

No white in sight.
Later, when I grew up,
I knew this was bad.
I only took the bus to go home.
I only sat at the front of the bus,
What's wrong with that?
I sat with white instead of black,
What's wrong with that?
I stood up for my colour of skin,
What's wrong with that?
I didn't want to sit at the back, of course, with black.
What's wrong with that?

Nothing.

Eva Rothlisberger (8)

My Mother

My mum had a stroke
When I was eight years old.
It was a normal day when she awoke,
And walked me and my sister to school,
As if nothing was wrong.

The day went and home time came,
But my mum wasn't where she belonged,
Things didn't seem the same
As my nan stood in her place.
I knew something was wrong.

We didn't go home that night
But my dad came around bearing news,
That on her brain something wasn't right;
A pale spot on the MRI.
Something was definitely wrong.

For a while I wondered;
Would she be the same?
I felt like my world was being plundered
To the ground.
Everything was wrong.

For a while my mum wasn't the same,
Unbalanced, un-synched, un-communicative,
It didn't seem right when she said my name,

In her slurred speech, trying her best.
But her best was still wrong.

A year came and went,
And when all seemed okay,
Another stroke came and went
All hopes crumbling down again.
Things would always be wrong.

But it was smaller than the last,
Leaving little damage in its wake,
Thankfully now it's in the past,
By nearly ten years.

My mum had a stroke when I was eight years old.
And again when I was nine.
But this hero of a mother is here to hold,
For many years from now, she will always be mine.

My mother.

Macy Hall (18)

Daddy Teddy

My daddy is like a big teddy bear,
he likes Skype and Google on his phone,
when we have dinner from Nando's,
he likes chicken with the bone.

He hides from me to smoke,
he loved Pakistani mango,
in the morning he says, "Ooo, hoo, I am late,"
and from work he brings sweets and Tango.

He is good at racing cars,
and he swims like a stone,
he likes to watch cricket matches,
but really hates to be alone.

He likes so many cups of coffee,
and to cook and eat spicy food,
every time we are together,
he is in a super mood.

When we fly high in the sky,
he makes sure I am fine,
he likes to meet politicans,
to talk and have a glass of wine.

After school we play football,
we run on the field and shout loud,

I am happy to show him my award,
my big teddy feels so proud.

At the weekend, when I meet him,
we master some nice drawing,
when I spend time with my daddy,
no, no, it is never boring.

It takes him almost an hour,
just to dress and to get ready,
sometimes he doesn't do what I want,
but I love so much, my Daddy Teddy.

Gabriel Haroon (7)

Hermione Granger

Hermione Granger is not a fool,
She gets top marks in every test in school.
Born on the 19th of September,
Didn't know she was a witch; if I remember.

Being a muggle-born is not easy,
People call them 'mudbloods', that is very cheeky.
In the Chamber of Secrets, Hermione liked being sneaky,
Stealing ingredients for the Polyjuice potion; the cupboard was creaky.

She also received a Time Turner from Professor McGonagall,
Time Turners can damage people and things easily, she had to be responsible.
After all that Time Turner subject fuss,
Hermione Granger decided to drop out of divination and all that muggle studies stuff!

She also made a Society of Elfish Welfare,
Hermione saw how the elves were treated, she had to make it fair!
She also helped organize Dumbledore's army,
If someone betrayed her, she wouldn't get all soft and marshy.

There are plenty more reasons about the successful Hermione,
From The Deathly Hallows back to Tom Riddle's diary.

Therefore, Hermione Granger is my narcissistic model,
From Harry Potter - my favourite novel!

Maria Abid (12)

Where I Want To Be

Who do I look up to?
Simple question, really.
Well, I'll answer it now,
Before I lose my sanity (nearly!)

Thinking now, there's nobody
I really want to be.
I don't look up to anyone
Except the future me.
However, there are some people,
That I envy, yet adore.
But then again, I look at them,
And wonder if I'm really sure.

Hurdlers really inspire me.
How do they jump so fast?
Having strength to run and jump,
Must take a strength that is vast!
I really like hurdles.
They are where I fit best.
I'd love to jump for England
In a red and blue vest!

I'm not sure of a lot of things.
Especially what I want to do.
One minute, I'd want to be a GP,
And the next, I wouldn't have a clue!

Coding sounds fun! It really does!
Like that woman, Roberta Something.
Making games for life made her rich!
Must've been a colossal win.

And then there's politics.
Theresa May!
Controlling the UK sounds
Like my type of day.
I'd need a great mentality
To fight for what is right.
Showing people reality,
And still looking bright!

In conclusion, there are lots
Of groups I look up to.
But there's nobody individual.
After all, your future is up to you!

Rebecca Obasuyi (13)

My Musical Idol - Shawn Mendes

The person whom I idolise and is my inspiration when I write is known to everyone worldwide.
A day doesn't go by when I don't think of what he means to me and why.
Whilst others are inspired by nature and events in the world; mine is the one I adore.
He inspires me through the music he writes.
His songs are extremely heartfelt;
I can't describe how happy I feel when I hear him day and night.

I love to write poetry and novels galore, but will now also try music as an avenue to peruse.
I will create my own style and flair,
In the hopes that I make it in the industry one day,
In the hopes that my music is loved by all.
I aspire to be like him,
Someone famous and renowned.
Who knows how far I will go.

I see the excitement and thrill he gets when he releases an album or performs on stage and want to do the same every day.
I see the courage he has to perform in front of thousands and the bravery that takes and aspire to do that myself, one day.

I would love for the chance for my music to be heard and received in the same way.
He is my inspiration to fulfil my dreams in the music industry and go further than anyone has ever gone before.

Jade Athwal-McNair (18)

Two Best Friends

Two best friends always there,
Two best friends always care,
They share and care, they are also kind,
They always have a thoughtful mind,
I don't know what to do with them,
Surely they are better than two men.
No one can break us apart,
Except our parents and our aunt
We have our way,
Even if we don't get through the day,
I still have two best friends
We will always make amends.

Two best friends always there,
Two best friends always care,
We know who we are,
I know you guys want a car
We are one with a star
The best thing belongs to us and that is school
We are really cool

Two best friends always there,
Two best friends always care,
They share and care, they are also kind
They always have thoughtful mind
I don't know what I'd do without them,

Surely they are better than two men.
They have hearts bigger than anyone else,
It will never melt!
They are made of fun things and happiness
Two best friends always there,
Two best friends always care
Two best friends!

Oluwatimilehin Deborah Kehinde (10)

Moons In My Night Soul

Moons in my night soul
Father knows the antidote to the poisonous pact
in my soul that feeds on my fears
Mother cooks the remedy to the scars left
by the past nightmares haunting reality
Mother soothes the broken world
through her calming, sweet lullaby
Father buys gold and castles
that transform me into a princess
then embraces my kingdom
and silently teaches me to be queen
Mother's earful nagging erupts the anger
twice the volume of yesterday
but those 'nagging' are concerns that rescue this naive child
who lives a fantasy
Father is mediating, fixing the problems
that segregate the family
understanding the tired eyes
opening the door of my soul
reassuring my self-love that drowned
Mother, a tender rose at times of my shuttered universe
and my strong shield at times of my wounded heart.

Both Mother and Father
Knights, queen and king, protecting their forever little princess

Lion and lioness forever shielding their little cub
Grateful words cannot express the love
Between I and them
Treasures that outdo anything in this world.

Mother and Father, moons in my night soul.

Satiya Bekelcha Yaya

My Idol - Nanny

My idol has changed through different times,
Depending on what life threw at me - lemons and limes.
My idol now has been with me throughout my life,
She even taught me how to use a knife!
My nanny is kind, that's easy to see,
She is somebody that everyone wants to be.
She's sweet and compassionate, yet can be strict too,
All of her friends would agree, especially Trisha and Sue!
Nanny is realistic, doesn't hide things away,
She always listens to what I have to say.
She sometimes makes mistakes, but doesn't cover them up with lies,
It's easy to get lost in her pretty eyes.
My nanny is my best friend, everyone knows,
I know that she's there for me, through the highs and lows.
When she visits New Zealand, to see her son
I miss her so much, I miss her a ton,
I love hearing about the things she has seen and done.
We've gone through a lot, yet she cares for me still,
There is never a time with her in which my happiness is nil.
I warn you though, she is *my* nanny,
If you mess with her you mess with both of us
I'll search every nook and cranny.

Ellie Webster (13)

Elizabeth Hamilton

Are you ahead of your time if your time is
being remembered?
You have probably passed someone with this person in
their heart,
Remembering her because she remembers him,
The man who tore her trust apart.

Elizabeth, you have what everyone should wish to have.
He must have rubbed off on you.
Your name is Hamilton - not only because of your marriage,
Because of all you went on to do.

You spoke against slavery, you kept Alexander's
flame burning.
All the while burning inside yourself, wishing he were there.
You, founder of New York's first private orphanage.
Like a bird, you sang his song, forgiving him the scandal you
had to bear.

His forked tongue whispering in someone else's ear.
He had no right to break the family like a mirror, pieces
shattered on the floor.
Seven years and more ending with a gunshot.
But first death took your son. His death reopened the door.

Elizabeth Hamilton, who repays you?
Burr lived, Alex died, you told his story.

Lola Gosling (13)

My Future Self

My future self,
A person who inspires me,
Is a question not to be answered trivially,
It's easy to get caught in the moment,
And answer with someone I don't even know well,
And though they might have played a part,
They didn't fully shape us into who we are,

Yet on the contrary,
Ironically,
It's easy to forget to say,
The people who inspire every day,
Those who work,
Try,
Sun or dirt,
And possibly only just get by,

That all said once again,
These people didn't mould us to become who we are in the end,
And sure their input might have helped in a way,
But giving credit where it's due is something we should also learn to say,
Even if it might seem conceited,
Its positive effects are not something to be rid,

In short, the person I idolise,
Is someone I'll know throughout my entire life,
A person who's learnt to change,
To thrive,
With a range,
Of feelings to stay living to the fullest whilst alive,

In happy times,
Through sad rhymes,
Even in sickness or health,
The person I idolise is the possibility of my future self.

Lucy Higgins

A Mother Like You

My heart is incomplete without you,
And the love can't be taken away.
I am following in your footsteps,
I know that's okay
Without a mother like you; I wouldn't know what to do
I would be going mad and even more sad
Without a mother like you

But who am I giving my love to,
Who could it be?
I love her more than anyone,
And that someone is you
And I'm sure she loves me too
Without a mother like you; I wouldn't know what to do

I would be going mad and even more sad
Without a mother like you
I know I have a dad, but that's not good enough
Because without you, I would be walking in a huff and a puff
I need you in my life; without you I cannot survive
If I didn't have you, I would struggle to be alive
Without a mother like you; I wouldn't know what to do
I would be going mad and even more sad
Without a mother like you; I wouldn't know what to do
I would be missing you so much and I know you would too!

Raniya Nazam Khan (8)

Mum

For all the things I have to say about the way I have felt along the way,
For all the times I haven't said 'thank you',
For all the words that have gone unspoken,
I love you for the way you stop and listen,
And your kind support through the years,
It's been a hard journey and I just would like to say thank you,
And if at times I am a trouble, you are always there,
And if at times I may have been ungrateful,
I don't know where you get the energy to be my mum and dad, maybe from your super porridge,
But there is something that is a beam of colours,
You tell me not to rub my face, but like every child I ignore you,
If I could give you diamonds for every tear you have shed for me, I think you would be a millionaire,
And if I could give you a pearl for every piece of wisdom you have shared with me, you could be a billionaire,
So, I would like to thank you for every piece of food you have given me and for the shelter you give me.

Sareena Padayachy (11)

My Amazing Mum

Every day I see her cleaning,
all the dishes are always gleaming.
The sweet aroma of the food,
helps me brighten my miserable mood!

She cares about our happy house,
to her kind-hearted and loving spouse.
She will always be in our dreams,
every day, in the dark, she will always beam!

She might be a good chatterbox,
but sometimes she's faster than a clock.
But still she is the amazing mum,
she's helpful and thoughtful all in one!

Mum is like a beautiful tree,
providing all the things for me.
She's always sweet just like honey,
her jokes are unmistakably funny!

She's the picture of perfection,
giving the right amount of affection.
She's as beautiful and pale as snow,
with rosy cheeks and a facial glow!

She tucks me in before she goes,
I close my eyes ready to doze.

She blows me a light and quick kiss,
which makes me express the feeling of bliss!

This is my amazing mum,
as she always heartens my downhearted glum!

Mariyam Tehseen (12)

Best Friends

Don't ever change for anyone
As you won't be loved by everyone
But you will always be my number one

Thank you for always being by my side
Even when I felt really upset and cried
For not leaving me based on other people's lies
For believing in me when others denied
Thank you for listening to my silent cries
And for not letting me be afraid and hide
But giving me courage to stand up and reply

You are one of a kind
You are very rare to find
And you're always in my mind
I know you will never leave me behind

You're the reason I smile
Even when I walk a mile
You're a beautiful flower
Which gives me power

You were the listening ear
When others were too busy to hear
You gave me your helping hand
When no one wanted to understand

You supported me when things got out of hand
And when I was not ready to take a stand

I wish you all life's joy
But will still be there to annoy
You're a dazzling, sparkling, glistening star
And I will always find you, no matter how far.

Mehmuna Kausar

A Flower Who Waters

A beautiful lady, who helps children grow if needed,
Walked into the greenhouse -
Only to see her plants had been deseeded.

Only one had learnt their English, science and maths,
As this child cared for her teacher, who led her down many different paths.

The others shrivelled back in their seats, unsure of what to do.
The teacher and the child gave them hints and they eventually came through.

The pens went on the paper, though for some no ink came out.
The duo helped them persevere even when they began to doubt.

The caterpillars grew into butterflies who flew away happy about their success.
They flew all the way to secondary - very eager to impress.

The girl and the teacher embraced whilst crying, for the girl had to depart.
The girl whispered to her helper,
"I'll never forget how you helped me - especially at the start."

"Your teachers will love you," said the teacher with a sigh,
And they embraced once more,
For them to say goodbye.

Bethan Worrall (11)

Inspiration

My angel, you're a rare type
No wings, no halo but a positive vibe,
A heart of gold, a soul so pure,
You're my idol, that I am sure.

Cruel words were spat at your face,
Cold daggers were shot your way,
But never once you complained;
Not a whimper, nor a sigh of pain,
With you only a smile remains.

My angel, you're a rare type
Not part of any hype,
With a burdened mind; a tired face
Trying to win an unpredictable race.
Bearing all thorns and storms of life,
All you ever did was strive.

Many efforts were in vain
A lot of pain you attained,
Many losses you endured
For the sake of us to be secure,
Forgiving all who betrayed,
For the happiness of those who stayed.

My angel, you're a rare type
No wings, no halo but a positive vibe,

A gift from God, a dad's love so pure,
You're my idol, that I am sure.

Areeb Tahira

Grandad, I Love You

Grandad,
The name says itself
A grand present given from God to me.

Your smile was made of gold,
Your eyes were full of stars,
You and Grandma
Were such comedy megastars.

Nothing can keep us apart,
Neither life nor death,
The smile on your face,
Now just a lasting memory in our hearts.

Your singing must have been pretty good,
For me to fall asleep,
You have always been the most loving, caring grandad,
The best there could be.

A hobby we shared
Was our love for movies,
And the movie nights we had
Will be in my heart forever.

Grandad, you were special,
You have a charming heart.
There will never be a grandad like you,
You will always have a special place in my heart.

I know you're up there,
Seeing me thrive,
You are the best grandad,
I miss you, Grandad,
I really, really do.

Rishika Raghunandanan

Jessica Ennis-Hill

J umping as high as she can to win a gold medal,
E very day she trains harder than anything,
S pinning round and round, trying her best to beat her discus score,
S he even got an MBE,
I njured in 2008, she missed out on Beijing, but then she was back on the track,
C alm at the start before the gun goes,
A chieved everything despite being bullied,

E ven though she's small, nothing will stop her,
N ever giving up is her thing,
N ow she has retired to spend time with her family
I n 2012 she won gold in London, her home nation
S he is so kind, she signed a photo for my birthday

H eptathlon is her sport,
I ndoor and outdoor athletics, she is still brilliant,
L ife has changed completely ever since she turned 13,
L eaping high in the air to beat her last record.

Fiona Jones (11)

I Love You!

M other
O h, my dearest companion of greatness
T aught me knowledge that if I hadn't known, would've been the biggest failure ever
H as a heart of pure light, so much that it rivals the sun
E ach time I shed a tear, she wipes it and gives me a warming hug
R oses are red, violets are blue, my mother is so beautiful that all of them will bloom

L ife would have been regretful without you
O f God's creation, you are among the best blessing and so is every other mother
V irtue honours you and I hope God honours you
E very way in which your feet walk, is like that of an angel

Y ou deserved to be honoured, Mother you deserved to be honoured
O h Mother, never will I abandon you, forgive me if I have wronged you
U nbroken is our bond and unchanged is our love.

Adam Faldeen Wareshallee (14)

My Poetry Idol

How amazing is her smile
Beautiful beyond description
Gradually shaping people's lives
Enticing beauty all around
A feminist who stood up for her rights
Making a small change and impacting the whole world
Her love is an ocean spreading itself
Passionate to care for the weak
No one is the same; everyone is uniquely different
She is a rainbow that outflows like magic in my eyes
My morning sun and wishing star
My blooming rose and dearest tree
She leads the way
Guiding me to the correct path
Working hard to become who she is now
A role model to me
Teaching me a lesson every day
I learn to love and care
Understanding the right way
Making progress every day
Although as humans, we mess up some days
But learn from our mistakes
Your past doesn't define you
It's what lies ahead that matters
Wow! This is the reflection of who she is

Always helping people
Making history every day
She is the one and only...

Meghan Markle
My Idol!

Eunice Opemipo Olagbolabo (10)

Figure Round The Bend

Across rubble roads, I spy him
Methodically wandering
Velvet coat falling to his sharp turn lightly
Elegantly sways like a swan out nightly
Calculated steps taken
Of polished shoes dazzling bright
He's everything I'm not and more
Am I good enough?

The confidence he possesses
For those scenarios he addresses
For he knows what to do
Knows what to say
The lively glint in his eyes when he talks
The calm posture as he walks
These little ditty things which drive me insane
Spotting him stroll the lane
He's everything I'm not and more
Puts me in a sway

His flawless faults are his undoing
But he knows how every trouble's brewing
The figure in my head. Too good to be.
Too good to exist in our reality
I may see him take sharp turns down the lane
Wishing I could be him someday

But I won't. I'm not him. And he's not me.
That's fine. I am good enough for me.

Michael C Hansell (17)

My Super Gran

Hair like a mad person, smile with a golden tooth,
When Granny arrives she is like a creature from Jupiter,
But I have a secret to tell you...
She's my sweet hero.
When my brother, Masimo, was born disabled,
She came to the rescue.
She left Albania quickly without saying a word.
She came and refused to leave, even if they put her in jail.
She was brave, fearless and intelligent.
She didn't speak a word of English, but she made friends with everyone on the bus, train, car, park.
She looked after Masimo non-stop for eight years.
When he didn't sleep at night, Granny was there.
When he was vomiting or constipated, Granny was there.
Her optimism is as powerful as her heart.
She always says Masimo will walk and talk.
She never gives up, like all heroes.

Xander Luca (7)

I Idolise My Mum

Idolise, admire and adore
Idolise, love and respect
I idolise my mum
Whenever I need her, she comes
Why, you ask?
There, here and everywhere, she has the talent to multitask

Idolise, love and respect
Idolise and admire
I admire and adore how her shoulders are empty for me to cry on
Arms open for me when I need comfort
To make me happy, the amount of effort
Hands free to help me up when I'm down
The determination for me to go on

I tell her jokes and she laughs
Always has a smile, even when things are tough
I can give you many more reasons, we will be here all day long
She says, "Life is not easy, you have to be strong."

Idolise who you love
Admire the one that makes your day
Idolise your mum is what I would say
Because, day or night you need her, she would stay...

Vishnupriya Ramamurthy

Remembrance

Grievers solemnly dug graves,
For those who were once brave,
Love is shown,
With no moan,
Remembrance for those who changed our lives.

Pushing through the earth,
Not breaking a law,
With all its might,
Poppies live through the time of war,
The fields fill with beautiful survivors,
Who in our heart are still great fighters.

An oath is taken,
While still shaken,
Silence,
Without violence,
Two minutes is all it takes,
Think of the impact it carefully makes.

I look up to them for,
They died for us,
With no fuss,
These life riskers are the best,
In heaven may they rest.

This is my inspiration,
Soldiers stood proud and tall,
Of course we love them all,
Nonchalant about their lives,
In their heads did they cry,
I'll remember them all my life,
I'll remember them with all my heart.

Thank you for being amazing.

Sophiyah Hannah Torabally (12)

My Magnificent Mother

There's one person who I love the most;
She's kind, helpful and she has always been there for me and always will be.

I've been with her since birth and I still am.
She is the best person I could ever know.

She is so clever, that sometimes I fall off my chair in surprise.
When she tickles me, she transforms into a comical clown.
Because she is so hard-working every day, she is like a role model for me.

When I'm feeling down, she comes and makes me feel up and joyful.
When I'm blue and lonely, she comes and makes me feel happy and not alone.

When I do something wrong, she makes it right.

Mum, I wish you knew how much you mean to me.
What an incredible mum!

Thank you!

Aysha Afridi (11)

My Idols

My friend Jenny is my idol
She's really kind and sweet,
She cheers me up when I'm feeling sad
She really can't be beat,

My mam is my idol
She makes perfect cups of tea,
She's supportive, just and loyal
She's the perfect mam for me,

My dad is my idol
He's helpful and smart,
He's the coolest person that I know
I love him with all my heart,

My little sister is my idol
She's inspiring and sweet,
I love it when we play together
It's always a huge treat,

I have many more idols
But I can only say a few,
I respect and look up to them
And I want to say, "Thank you!"

Abigail Lewis (12)

My Grandpa Pig

Saturday was my favourite day of the week,
You and Granny would come,
To play games that were always unique.

Peppa Pig was always on my mind,
Grandpa Pig was your new name,
but you didn't like it because I made you act.

Years went by,
and height was our competition,
it was my mission.

Life was great,
perfect,
till one day,

Cancer,
but with us at your side,
you were sure to win.

One sunny day in April,
everything looked fine,
then I realised,
you were no longer mine.

You had grown wings in my sleep,
to Heaven you must go,
I miss you with all my heart, Grandpa Pig,

Without you, our games are history,
one long memory,
I love you, Grandad,
you were my energy.

Not a day goes by,
when you are not in my head,
love in my heart,
or tears that are shed.

Ysabella Jo Strudwick (14)

My Auntie Linda

(Linda Margaret Blades 23/09/1959-05/09/2018 Aged 58. Sorely missed xx)

My lovely auntie was Linda Blades
My memories of her will never fade
I will always remember her as a little adventurous
She loved her family, she was very generous
She was my hero, she was very courageous
When she got cancer, she had treatment in different stages

When she was ill, we went on caravan holidays
We had lots of fun in many different ways
We visited lots of interesting places
And kept all our clothes in the suitcases

When she died aged 58
I was lost, she was like my best mate
She was my shoulder to cry on when times were bad
She gave kind words and hugs when I was sad
Auntie Linda was such a chatterbox
She was the best and I loved her lots.

I'm hoping everyone can see
Just how much she means to me.

Kathryn Blades (11)

My Mum

My mum may seem quite normal to people other than me
She is polite and nice and makes a lovely tea
But when she takes me home from school...
She splashes in the swimming pool
She juggles like a clown at the fair
She dyes the whole rainbow in her hair
Last night she made a wedding cake for the Queen
The best for miles around to be seen
She fights criminals with the police
She can make a fluffy woollen fleece
My mum can sail around the world
She can get her hair perfectly curled
She can sing opera in Sydney
So now you can definitely see
My mum is such a great superhero
But that is not why I love my mum, no
It's because when she cuddles me at night,
She says, "Don't let the bedbugs bite!"

Margot Grand (10)

The Greatest Friend

With a secret smile and tear-filled eyes,
Getting to know her soul is a hidden surprise.

You'll never realise you need her until she's gone,
But by that time she has picked up her things and peacefully moved on.

Filled with compassion, honour and love for those near,
I wish she knew how valued she was here.

Earth and life can be dangerous, envious and overall unfair.
She teaches me lessons she didn't realise was there.

So when you meet this girl, don't just smile and nod,
She was put on Earth by almighty God.

She is a rose and she will grow thorns,
But can bring out warmth to help others with their remorse.

Asia Shaddad (19)

Proud To Have A Papa Like You

You are like the sycamore tree,
Protecting and caring for me free.
You are so large, never keeping me apart,
Symbolising your kind and warm heart.
For me, you are the North Star,
As from my heart you are never far.
Leading the way, you are always day and night,
Shining like a luminous and bright light.
For me, you are God's messenger,
Telling me to never give up and to try harder and harder.
Showing me the wrongs and the rights,
You add to my life more and more lights.
You are and will always stay as my hero,
For you are the one whose footsteps I will follow.
I am thankful to God for having sent such a dad,
Who I cannot even imagine saying anything bad.
Thank you, God, for having sent a dad.

Gurleen Gupta

My Lovely Mum!

At day and night,
I love my mum
And she loves me too
I hope I can be like her
Brave and kind
Smart and funny.

She cooks better than the rest
She is a better mum than I wished
I love her
She loves me too
Days turn to weeks,
Weeks turn to months
And months turn to years
She loves me
And I love her
She is my idol.

She helps me
She is a great person
And no matter what
I would like to be like her
Because
I adore her
She is my idol.

She gives me fun
She is the best
My mum is as brave as a lion
And dances better than I think
I love her
I adore my mum.

Noemi Kufera (9)

DanTDM

He is very popular
as you may think.
'Cause he dyes his hair blue
and occasionally pink.

He got a part as Eboy
in 'Wreck-It Ralph 2'.
He searches stuff on Google
but never Yahoo.

He has long hair
and a very short beard.
But that doesn't stop him
from playing games that are weird.

He gives lots of challenges
to all of his fans.
He is very short
and has no caravans.

TDM stands for
The Doodling Monkey.
Or is it for something else?
Anyway, it's funky.

Okay everybody
this is the end.

Make sure you stay happy
and subscribe to DanTDM!

Joseph Lawrence (9)

Dad, You Are My Idol

I love you, Dad,
You work so hard every day and night,
Always helping me to do things right,
Your kind-hearted nature makes you special,
You are more than just my dad,
You are my idol,
Patience is what you have best,
No matter what I do wrong you always forgive me,
When you leave I feel disheartened,
But when you come back I feel enlightened,
You are so generous in everything you do,
I really wish I could be like you,
After all those things you do for me every day
I will do the same to you one day,
I am so proud of you and your work,
I will always look up to you,
I love you, Dad, to the moon and back.

Imethma Weerarathna

Soldiers

S aviours of the world, where would we be without soldiers?
O utstanding, brave and courageous, going out to an horrendous place like war, risking their own lives to save ours.
L ife savers, many dead or injured to make sure we are happy, safe and free.
D edicated and determined to set their country and people free and bring peace to the world.
I nspiring men and women to fight for their country. They are truly incredible and important to our world.
E ncouraging young people to fight for freedom, bringing hope and confidence.
R emarkable for their bravery and strength.
S incere, splendid, smart soldiers will never let us down.

Denny Kurera (14)

Cousins? More Like Brothers!

I absolutely love my cousin.
He makes me die of laughter,
And saves all the food till after.
I call him baiyah*, not only because I'm Bengali,
But it's rude to say his name,
After all, I'm not lame!
We are both in it to win it,
And we are there for each other,
Did I mention we are like brothers?
We play games and have fun,
We occasionally have bread buns.
Add a cup of tea,
And we will be full of glee.
We also play football,
And always smash the ball into the fence
Because the matches are very tense.
One day I want to be like him,
Intelligent, hilarious and be rich with friends.
After all, our brotherly bond will never end!

(*means brother in Bengali).

Rezwan Islam (11)

My Dad

My dad's temper spreads as quick as fire on wood,
He helps me with my projects and that's always good,
My dad is fun but always on his phone,
He forces us to eat good things for your bone.

He's the one who takes us shopping to buy,
And the one who's good at DIY,
He makes us laugh but is always out,
Never cooks and the dishes mount.

In the night he snores lots and lots,
But puts the plants from our garden into pots,
As he's my dad, I love him,
He makes our lights never get dim.

My dad is clever and very, very strong,
Generous, reliable, and never ever wrong,
He helps everyone but shies away from fame,
When I grow up, I want to be just the same!

Sneha Daga (13)

Idolisation

It never really crossed my mind,
Who an idol could be.
I just assumed it was someone popular, admired,
But I wasn't quite right, you see.
I thought hard about this,
An idol... What to look for...
Then suddenly, it hit me hard,
It's about their qualities.

An idol is someone who cares.
An idol is someone you aspire to be.
An idol is someone who is ever supporting.
An idol is someone who works hard, behind the scenes.

They don't have to be famous,
They don't have to be 'most talented'.
Sometimes, you don't even acknowledge them,
Yet they carry on,
Supporting you every day.
A superstar in their own way.
Always there for me,
Mum.

Nicole Zheng

My Idol

Who would it be?

Would it be a fictional charcter, who saves lives,
In a friendly neighbourhood... Spider-Man perhaps?

Or... Should it be a real-life character, who changed the world,
In a technological way... Bill Gates perhaps?

Wait a second!
Why look so far and wide?
When he's right by my side.

Naanu... I call him,
My mum's dad,
My grandad!

He's generous and kind,
As he helps the mute, deaf and blind.

Not just that, he's also clever,
And succeeds at every endeavour.

So Naanu is my hero,
As he came up from zero!

Rohun Manarkattu

My Idol Is...

My idol is my mum,
She is kind, caring and a fun woman
When I need her the most she is there.
When I'm upset she is too,
And when I'm happy she is too!
And I'm really grateful
To have her as a mum!

My idol is my mum
Yes, she can get on my nerves sometimes
But that's what family is right?
We laugh together, we suffer together
Whether good or bad
And that's my mum,
She is amazing!
We share good memories,
And bad ones too
But most importantly
We have fun together.

I love my mum
And she loves me too!
I want to be like her
When I grow up
Because she is wonderful

I couldn't ask for a better mum
Than the one I already have here!

Simisola Nancey Majekodunmi (12)

Channy Thompson

The 24th of March 2018 in Hexham
I heard you sing for the first time.
I was speechless,
You're gorgeous, talented and inspiring.
You're kind, caring and inspirational,
Nobody I would rather look up to than you,
You believe in me, you told me to go for it,
When I said I wanted to become an actress.
I don't believe in me, nobody else does
But you do,
I am going to follow my dreams for you
And do it,
You're my rock,
My idol,
The only reason I smile these days.
You show people that you can do anything,
If you put your heart into it.
I have autism and don't normally like loud music, but yours is different.
You are my idol today and forever.

Beth Anderson (15)

My Favourite Cousin

I have a cousin who is sweet and kind.
We always have fun together.
We always read books together.
I love her so much that she is my favourite cousin.
She goes to the shops and gets what we really want.

If I am ever bored, we play board games.
She is one intelligent woman.
We always take pictures wherever we go.
She takes us on nice trips which makes me happy.
One of the trips we went on was to the water park.

She inspires me by her intelligence.
If I am ever sad, she will be there for me.
My cousin and I always have a laugh.
She makes us nice food to eat.
Which I think is really nice and delicious.
Both of us like to draw, watch films and read books.

Habiba Begum

The Light That Creates A Shadow

I can feel you in your touch,
I can feel you from your smile.
But mostly I know I can't see you for a while.
I know you raised me, taught me, loved me;
But you never taught me this:
Not being able to feel you in your touch,
Your smile being wiped.

You never taught me the coldness of your skin and
When I say, "You're gone" - I feel you
- Not by touch
But by the light and I see you in my shadow.
You're never gone, this is for you.

I see the smile you gave me in the mirror,
I see you everywhere and nowhere.
I love you, and I know deep down -
You never left me.
I can still feel you.
We'll meet again,
This I know.

Madeleine Francesca Lake

VooDoo

VooDoo is my favourite wrestler and he fights for WrestleForce.
He is taller than a giant and stronger than a horse.
They play his creepy music when he walks into the room.
He flips over the ropes and lands on his bum and the room echoes loudly with a boom.
He has his face painted like a skull and has a blue tongue and plait in his hair.
His enemy is waiting in the ring petrified because VooDoo makes everyone scared.
He starts the fight with a grab around his neck, let the battle begin.
He punches, kicks and body slams, VooDoo is going to win!
VooDoo is my hero, my idol and my friend.
I can't wait to see him when he is in the wrestling ring again.

Olivia Lambert (10)

Ariana Grande

A mazing Ariana, the best there is,
R esilient, a hater won't bring her down,
I nspirational, the one you look up to,
A ctress, playing all the best bits,
N egotiable, it is not all about her,
A dmiring, come on, you know one has the most talent!

G orgeous, one of the prettiest there,
R espectful, respects the fact that other people are better.
A spirational, everybody loves her,
N ever holds back,
D ecisive, you can rely on her to make choices,
E xciting, this powerhouse always brings a mesmerising show!

Grace Eighteen (9)

Aunty

Mother's Day for me, is futile, so let's change it.
Instead I write this to another - my aunty.
That may be different from what you ask, I admit
I can't do the spoken word, so to this my words apply.
So Mother's Day? No. But a woman in your life? Yes.

Maybe I don't consider her a mother, but does it matter?
After all, there's children with no parents,
But can still care for another.
When together there's a lot of chatter.
So to this I want to make everyone more aware
And I won't say Mother's Day, for other women can be the ones who we admire.

Claire Lucy Gee (18)

How I Like My Mum!

My mum is pretty and witty
She makes me smile all the time
She smells like roses and candyfloss posies
And she's all mine.
My mum is good at helping out, although sometimes she messes about.
My mum is a fantastic cook in every way
And I'd like to say, she likes it this way.
My mum is a good driver, although she doesn't like it that way
My mum plaits her hair with a great big bow, that's how I like it that way
I like the way my mum dresses, always in her besties
I like your hugs, they're like you're being hugged by a big fluffy bear who really cares
That's how I love my mum and I will always stay that way.

Colby Lewis Blackborow

My Mum

M y mum is the best
Y ou can only dream of having a mum like mine

M orning after morning she cares for me
U nder no circumstances does she forget me
M any people would love a mum like mine

I ntelligent is what she is
S he is very special to me

A mazing doesn't even begin to describe her
M y idol, my best friend, my mother
A ll of those things above are what she is
Z any is one way to describe her
I nfinite love for my mum I have
N ever-ending care for me she provides
G reat mother and friend who cares a lot.

My idol who I love so much.

Shania Miah

Guess Who?

Have you ever met that person who you just love?
A person you love with all your heart,
Their faults and flaws, all the above.
You know, that kind of love that never departs.
Have you ever met a person who cares for you?
A person who always tells you the truth,
No matter what you're going through.
A person who embraces life like a youth.
Have you ever met a person who loves you regardless?
Someone who is always by your side,
Especially in your times of darkness.
Step by side, stride by stride.
Have you ever met that person who makes your heart beat like a drum?
Fortunately, I have and that person is my mum.

Deborah Esan

Who I Idolise

Who I idolise is smart and very cool,
I think my idol might know all,
They have amazing taste in style,
So shopping takes a while,
But then again, I do love the mall.

Who I idolise is extremely kind,
The idol helps people who are sadly blind,
They love to read and draw,
Are astonishing at law,
If only you were in court you could've saw.

Who I idolise gives me a lot of knowledge,
Things you learn in college,
I hope they get more acknowledged,
They're also not an alcoholic,
As well they are very symbolic.

My idol is the best, better than the rest, but who do you think my idol could be?

Tanisha Zaman (12)

My Poetry Idol: The Duchess Of Cambridge

My poetry idol is pretty
She is also incredibly witty
I admire that she is so graceful
Not a stitch of her clothing is dull
She is a strong woman but still gentle
There's nothing in the world she couldn't handle
Every day she is perfectly kind
A match for her wisdom would be hard to find
As a mummy she is very devoting
Joy, grace and happiness is what she brings
She has a keen interest in photography
Like me, it makes her feel happy
She is so bright and positive
A way that we could all live
I wonder if she ever makes late trips to the fridge?
My poetry idol is the Duchess of Cambridge.

Katie Adeosun (12)

My Idol...

Is it my mum and stepdad who are always there?
Is it my sister who I love dearly?
Or my stepbrother could it be?
Or even my closest friends?
There isn't one, or even two,
If you're in my life, this is for you!
They're not all in my family tree,
It's everyone who surrounds me!
We share the laughter and the tears,
And I even told them my darkest fears,
We've all been in doubt,
When we're together, we can work things out!
A combination of these people in my life is vital,
As together they all make up my idol.

Alicia Geere (11)

Albert Einstein - The True Hero

A mazin' he is,
L ogical he always has been,
B elieving he did,
E ffort he put in,
R eaching for his goal,
T rusting himself on the way!

E ndeavour he had to do,
I nspiring he is to everyone,
N ot knowing where his path would lead to,
S till he kept trying,
T errific he is,
E instein created a new world,
I f not for him, we wouldn't be living how we are,
N ow let's take a moment to appreciate what Albert Einstein did for us!

Ella-Mai McKitten (8)

Inspired By Mum...

She shouts, she screams,
Only because
She wants me to fulfil my dreams.

She's been with me
From the start,
And never ever
Will we be apart.

I admire her
Style, clothes, shoes and bags,
As long as she looks good
It doesn't matter about the price tags.

Inspiring,
Admiring,
Always to and fro,
She is always there for me
And never lets go.

They say,
Mothers are a daughter's best friend,
Which is true
Because she's with me
From beginning to end.

Eisha Miah (11)

Uncle John

You have been in my life for as long as I remember
We have always been together
Rock by rock, side by side
Uncle and niece, it has always been right
Being the best male role model I've got
It sure is a lot on your shoulders
Though you never ever show it,
You are my uncle after all
I'm so glad to have your love best of all,
You're my uncle John, the tallest of all
But always in my life you will remain
'Cause Uncle John, my heart you never have to gain
For being in my life is all I ask for you to remain.

Lucyanne Reid

My Great Mother

M y great mother Sultana,
Y oung, pretty, wearing henna.

G iving us all unconditional love,
R esponding to our needs like a dove.
E ach of us have great appreciation,
A ll of the time she's paying us attention.
T he most warmth, compassionate and caring,

M y great mother is not for sharing.
O ver the rainbow I may travel,
T ime will eventually reveal,
H ighs and lows of life's great deal.
E ach night I hope and pray,
R espectfully for the wellbeing of my great mother every day.

Sharmili Fatema (10)

My Idol

She is an inspiration
To all the nations
Out there
She is fair
She has long hair
Where there is a tear
She will wipe away
She will always make you happy
Even when she's snappy
She believes that the world should be just
To do so
She makes videos
To teach everyone
How it should be done
She wants everyone to be treated equally
And for them all to have decency
She has many inspiring sayings
And with her crew
#teamsuper
She spreads awareness
That there should be
Fairness
Everywhere
She is a comedy star
Which is bizarre

As she is also a
YouTuber
Author and an actress!

Femy Biju (10)

My Granda

It made me so very happy
When I was only two
That my mum and I got a house
So very close to you
I remember all the good times
And all the laughs we shared
But when it came to losing you
I certainly was not prepared
I'll think about you every day
And how you were so strong
You fought so hard and were so brave
And you did it for so long
You really were one in a million
A cut above the rest
All who knew you would agree
You simply were the best.

Love you big dodds Granda, love Leah xx

Leah Weston (13)

Family Poem

Jel:
The laughter, the happiness, the joy you bring,
The smiles you give, I just can't keep in,
You bring the light that is lost, and make our family complete.
Everyone has a dad, but no one has a Jel!

Mum:
You are as precious as gold, I will cherish forever,
I love you and care for you like no other,
You are my one and only perfect mother,
Everyone has a mum, but none are like mine!

Brother:
As cute as a teddy bear
You are shiny and new
My cuddles show just how much I love you!

Grace Kirkham (10)

My Mum

My dear mother, you are the best
Truly better than the rest
You always put me first
Even when I'm at my worst

Through all your hardships, you never stopped
Even when your precious items dropped
I cried, I cried all night and day
Sometimes you had no time to lay

You cook, you work, you still have time for me
Also when I got stuck in the tree
From birth till now, I know I'm the special one
With you I always have fun.

I love you, I love you, I truly do
There's no need for someone new
You give me all the love I need
And I honestly mean it.

Rabia Islam Chowdhury

Mother

You have always been beside me,
through the ups and downs in life,
you have always reassured me,
always helped me get through pain and strife.

I always wondered why,
why you stayed with me,
even after countless arguments,
you were always happy as can be.

Now I know why and it wasn't just for show,
it was because of your dear, big heart
and love for me, now I know.

Mother, I am sorry,
sorry for all the times I hurt you bad,
I just want you to know that I love you
and you're the best mom anyone could have ever had.

Noor-Ul-Ain Bhatti (15)

Best Mum Ever

My mum is kind, thoughtful and nice.
She always helps me from burning days,
And she is the best mum I could ever wish for.

My mum always gets stuff I want,
But sometimes parents can be a little harsh.
She fills my days with rainbow light,
Fairy tales and sweet dream nights,
And then in love she set me free.

Me and my brothers are mischief-makers,
But like the moon and the stars, she takes care of us,
And in my dreams you are the star.
My mum is a superhero to me.

Elham Alizadah

Super-Mum

Super-Mum,
Super-Mum,
Where are you now?
Had five kids,
I don't know how,
Been through so much, yet still here,
Always, always, always near,
Always caring like you've made a pact,
Never embarrassing, that's a fact.

Super-Mum,
Super-Mum,
Where are you now?
To the kitchen, super pow!
I guess I've inherited your powers,
Finally I've found you after about one hour!
I knew for sure you were near,
Wait, is that dinner I hear?

Jameela Mansour (13)

Author

An idol
Is someone you are meant to look up to
To fantasize about
Their life
Or being in their life
I have two:
Paula Hawkins
And E. Lockhart
I want to write like them
I want the readers to feel that connection towards my characters
As I imagine being
Rachel, Anna or Megan
Or maybe Cadence, Mirren or Gatwick
I wonder if I
Could step into their worlds
Each one so unique
And so vibrant
And complicated
Like life
And all you have to do to enter
Into these worlds
Is look at words on a page
And immerse yourself into the story...

Leah Mae Wilkes (12)

My BFFs

My BFFs are there to help me,
Anywhere or anytime.
When I feel sad,
They make me laugh.

My BFFs always listen to me,
They respect me and care for me.
They take care of me,
When I feel ill.

My BFFs are always there for me,
In the good or bad.
If we fall out,
It's only over silly things.

My BFFs are sometimes silly,
And make me laugh at their jokes.
They play with me and never leave me out,
So I think I have really nice BFFs.

Amelia May Lacey (8)

My Idol

Liam Gallagher is just one of those guys,
The person I idolise.
I like many other people, but after all,
Liam is my Wonderwall.
One of his new songs is called 'When I'm in Need',
It's a brilliant song, very good indeed.
I also like 'Wall of Glass',
I think about it when I'm in class.
Another one is 'Universal Gleam',
It's about fixing your broken dream.
It will give you something to shout about,
Liam won't ever let us down.

Tyler Jessop (15)

Theresa May

Is the best of the best
each new day she faced
a new threat,
but like a test,
she overcame
from fighting a cold
to losing the polls
all for the people's votes.
They made fun,
shared peers
but she still rose like the sun
and set like the night
while we all whined
she continued to fight.
When the EU fought back up
until she practically got the sack.
She was packed with courage,
packed with might
until she lost the fight.

Trey Devonte Mclean (16)

J.K. Rowling

J.K. Rowling writes the best books.
Keeping Harry Potter great even on the eighth.
Reading it is so much fun.
How can it be better?
Her books fit together like a jigsaw.
I love every book you write, they keep me awake at night.
Seeing you write is quite a sight.
I know people can read them all.
Reading them is just a ball.
No author better than Harry Potter's best-selling author.
How great it is to write about you.
You are my idol, you really are.

Georgina Neillings (9)

She's Magic

My idol is good at writing,
Her books are very exciting.
There's wizards and magic,
The ending's never tragic.
I bet there's a light bulb in her head,
Every time she goes to bed.
She writes lots and lots and lots,
But one idea never rots.
Expelliarmus is a spell,
Does this ring a bell?
From one adventure to another,
There's always a mystery to uncover.
With a wave of your wand and a great big whizz,
Do you know who she is?

Charlie Caine (7)

Suffragettes Rule Like All Of Us

Persevering, never giving up
Trying not to feel empty like a cup
Spirits held high
Head lifted above
As eager as a newborn pup

Relying not only on luck
Not listening to men saying they suck
Spirits held high
Head lifted above
Not afraid of a bit of muck

Moving forward, going on
Dancing by singing their song
Spirits held high
Head lifted above
Going on a parade so long

Working together so happily
Playful but passionate gleefully
Spirits held high
Head lifted above
Suffragettes rule like all of us.

Lucy Arnold (11)

Grandma

My idol's a person that you cannot see,
My idol's a person who inspires me,
My idol's a person I will continue to love,
Although they're up in Heaven above.
Without this person my life is sad
But working like this would make them so glad
If only this person could see
The impact that they had on me.
My life will continue though they are not here
Knowing they're watching fills me with cheer,
But nobody believes things they can't see
Things like the love of my idol from me.

Olivia Morrell (15)

Not A Single Idol

Many people I know aspire,
But as for me, an idol is hard to acquire,
You see, there's just too many to count,
Like trying to see through mist,
But anyways, I'll give you a list.

First up is my sister, sometimes sweet,
Or sore like a blister.
Next is Mum, head of the house,
She even helped me rescue a woodlouse!
Finally, it's Dad, playful and funny,
Though at the end of the day, he's Mama's honey.

So that's all from me and my pen,
How about you read this all again?

Evie O'Meara (11)

Julia, My Sister

J oyful every day
U nderstanding when I need her
L oves me as I love her
I ncredible at singing
A mazing at cooking

M y very best friend
Y ou would really like her to be your sister

S isters forever
I n feelings she is very kind
S o special in every way
T alented in learning
E ncourages me when I'm sad
R eady to do anything for me.

Karolina Mrozinska (8)

Beautiful Smile That I Know

An amazing person that I know,
A beautiful smile and eyes that glow,
Personality that's always great,
Hoping she won't change.

She is always here and everywhere,
Supporting me anywhere,
Even through the hard times,
She is always by my side.

Nothing will ever change,
Everything will always stay the same,
She will never let me down,
Even when I have a breakdown.

A beautiful smile that I know,
That I will never let go,
My mum will always try,
She will never be unqualified.

Joanna Majchrzyk (13)

My Idol... David Walliams

Me and my author,
Link together like a cup and saucer.

And being funny,
Makes him a lot of money.

He was inspired by his granny,
Me too, I was helped by my nanny.

He also writes books,
And knows just where to look.

His ideas are crazy,
Make my brain all hazy.

We were both born in August,
He had to change his name.

We learnt to trust,
Do you think life will ever be the same?

Amelia-Jane Charleton (8)

Mother Knows Best

Mother, Mother you know best
That's what sets you apart from the rest
You can help me with what I need
That's what probably makes you see
The annoying girl I always have been

Don't let me go
You need to help me
And you will see
My love for you is and always will be

Mother, Mother you know best
You save me from the world
When I need help
You're like a dictionary in class, always there when I need you

For what it's worth
Mother, Mother you know best.

Khadija Ajmal (13)

Why My Mum Is Special

Roses are red,
Violets are blue,
I love nothing except for you,
You teach me not to be rude,
Even in a whole afternoon,
You took my hands,
And helped me understand,
All different things all unplanned,
Now all thanks to you,
My imagination grew,
To be something wild and new,
And it's all thanks to you,

Just like a flower,
She gives me the power,
To shower my knowledge,
Even over a hedge.

Alesha Akhtar (11)

Mum And Dad

Mum
You are the sun that shines in the skies
Like the diamonds in your eyes
You held my hand when times got tough
Been by my side when life got rough
I love you more than words can say
Even until today.

Dad
I love you, Dad
You cheer me up when I am sad
You are the lock that keeps me safe
That nobody can break
You are the diamond glints on snow
I just wanted to let you know
And I love you so.

Holly Ferns

My Family

My dad is a lion
His shouts are his roars
Sometimes he has fights
And he walks out the doors

My mum is an angel
She really is ace
I love my mummy
So much
For the smile on her face

My sister is a monkey
She jumps all around
She's hyper most of the time
And rolls on the ground

My brother is a panda
With round and rosy cheeks
I am a koala
And I can sleep for weeks.

Hakeem Hafidz

J.K. Rowling

J.K. Rowling says Sirius is prowling,
In the corridors of Grimmauld Place.
So, if you hear howling, he is very much owling Professor
Lupin or Snape.

J.K. Rowling is quite profounding
And inspires everyone to write.
If I ever meet her, I would ask her
What makes a good book to write?

J.K. Rowling made a potion that
Makes you feel every emotion.
So with a pinch of magic, a dash of adventure
And a scatter of luck... *Kaboom...!*
She got the recipe right.

Aditi Bilawar (9)

Best Friend

Harley Moore,
You have always been kind,
And always been there for me,
You've built up my character,
And made my face shine with glee,
You've killed my grief,
And then made me smile,
You've eased my pain,
I dread to say goodbye to you in a while,
Best friends for life,
The memories we've had,
Good and funny times,
You are a good lad,
You go to one school, I go to another,
Our friendship will end,
Never will I forget you,
Farewell, best friend.

Mohamed Awadalkarim (11)

Martin Luther King

There are many inspirational people in the world,
But his name struck first in my mind,
The man who had a dream,
The one who wanted peace,
Opportunity did he seize,
He went to a segregated school,
Where he was used as a tool,
Part of the Civil Rights Movement
And made a great improvement,
Books, speeches, protests,
And it led to the best,
There are many inspirational people in the world,
But his name struck first in my mind,
His name, Martin Luther King.

Atheesh Ramesh (14)

Katie Archibald

The wind in her hair,
Everything's aero,
Cheers everywhere,
She is my hero!

On track and road,
Sweat, blood and tears,
Pedal mode,
Encouraging cheers.

In her mind's eye
The gold medal awaits,
You sprint or you die
Like you love or you hate.

Criterium on road,
Omnium on track,
On she rode,
She couldn't go back.

One day race,
Or Grand Tour,
Madison chase,
And lots more.

And so she hurtles across the line,
Taking with her the winning time.

Grace Upshall

My First Friend

My mother was my first home, but you were my first friend
We were never introduced to one another, but I knew who you were
I'd seen you before
In the mirror.

Slowly we grew closer and day by day you became more familiar with me.
You learnt that I really liked hard-boiled eggs
And I quickly learnt that you were lactose intolerant

You put effort into those things, that much I do remember
And you still do.
And guess what?

You always will.

Cece Anang

The Idol That Inspired My Creations

The star of my life
Giving me felicitous, jocular joy
It brings me strength
Holding back my honing anger
The apple of my eye
It dances beatifically on the moon
Throwing literature and luck
When anyone is despaired
The two primary things unite
To form a powerful mixture of work and fun
My idol is
A fantastic, bombastic...
Author
Wouldn't you even subtly agree?

Jasper Collins (10)

Mother

She cares for you, day,
Till night.
Pulls the monsters from under,
The bed.

Finds a way to help,
Us out.
She loves us,
Morning till night.

She's always up for a cuddle,
And a snuggle.
When you're down she picks,
You up.

We love you, Mother,
We love you,
You're our idol,
Through and through.

Through the hard times you,
Cuddle us and through,
The happy, you cry for us,
We love you.

Goodnight, Mother,
God bless.

Poppy Tester

Me And My Grandad

I love my grandad because he is kind and sweet,
And he sometimes buys me yummy treats.

He is tall and strong,
But he doesn't like loud songs that go

Bong!

My grandad collects me from school,
And he waves and smiles at me
When I am in the swimming pool.

I love my grandad because he is full of love,
But most of all, he gives the best hugs!

Gia Oubhie (5)

Blue Eyes

I'm scared
But he makes me want to do it
When he laughs, I laugh
"Be the best," he says
My mind says how
My heart says I am
My future is his heart
My past is his mind
Going through life with him makes me want time to never end
The times he's away makes me neutral
Makes my head go round the bend
Blue eyes make it seem like an ocean
I am grateful for the hard things he does for me
You are loved
I am.

Lily McElroy (10)

Abigail

Abigail, Abigail
I love you,
You're a great gamer
And I am too.

Abigail, Abigail
Give me a squeeze,
Let's get in bed
With spaghetti and cheese.

Abigail, Abigail
You're the best,
There's so much to play
Give me a rest.

Abigail, Abigail
You're a great sister,
I need to ask you
Why do we never play Twister?

Evelyn Louise Brandt (8)

My Sister, Delilah!

My little sister, Delilah,
Is such a little smiler,
She's always getting into trouble
My mum's forever saying she's my double.
I love my sister oh so much
Especially her hugs, kisses and touch.
We will be best friends forever
She is so beautiful and so clever.
As long as I have a sister
I will forever have a best friend.
Together forever until the very end.

Ava Dobie (9)

Gigi Hadid

G rateful and blessed are her secret possessions
I ntriguing with her selection of new Reebok footwear
G hostly as she haunts people in their dreams
I ndigo lipsticks are what she rarely wears

H ungry for FAO Schwarz red military jackets
A stonishing personality
D aringly supplementing her looks
I ntroverted not so often
D eathly luring in the modelling industry.

Momina Khan

Daddy

Every day he plays with me,
Helps me learn and makes me see,
That when I grow up, I can be whatever I wanna be,
He is very caring even when things are bad,
I mean you know he's the best dad...
All around the world you would know,
He is the best dad, high or low.
When we are at home, he will help me make
Or even sometimes bake,
He's a great dad... the best dad.

Molly Charlton (9)

Rose

Like a rose
That blooms throughout
Winter, summer, spring

And autumn, each petal
A perfect shade of pink
Harmony, peace and love

Beauty with a beast
Wilted with a slow shade of grey
But within the core, the love will stay

And I know I may never tell you
But I really, really do
Even in the darkest of times, know that
I love you.

Israt Orpa Ahmed (13)

Tyler Joseph Idol Poem

I listen to your music
Every day
Not missing or leaving any to stray
It gives me life
Every time
Playing it is mine

I listen to your music every week
After hard hours
I always have this
To rely on
When things get bleak

I listen to your music
Every month
Something I always look forward to
I see it as my reward.

Emily McGhee (14)

My Mother

You guide me through my life and help me avoid obstacles when it's rough,
You take care of me and make sure that I don't fall when things are tough,
You teach me to understand the difference between what appears good and what is truly good,
And also you feed me delicious food with the main ingredient love,
This is my life's sum,
That you are my caring mum.

Shona Pandey (10)

Besty Westy

I see your wrongs, I see your rights
Then you start shining bright
You're my Besty Westy.
Sometimes we argue, sometimes we don't,
I love you Besty Westy
When I fall, you help me up,
You're my favourite Besty Westy.
We have a little giggle like we are Besty Westys
Nothing changes between us
You're just my Besty Westy.

Jessica Beck

The Most Amazing Mum Of The Earth

The most amazing mum of the Earth is mine,
And helps me lots in my rather mysterious life,
She cooks me meals,
She cleans my clothes,
She keeps me warm
And buys a car to take me home.
I'm very lucky to live with her,
She's my inspiration and my heart is hers,
All the girls in despair take a quick look around and appreciate.

Sophia Hussain

To My Mum

Your beautiful blonde hair shines like diamonds on the beach
Your skin is wonderfully soft like a pretty peach
Your eyes blue, like the sea
You work hard, like a honeybee
You pull me up when I'm down
You're really not a red-nosed clown
You give me luck when I have none
Your smile is brighter than the sun
Thank you, Mum!

Chiara Gavazzi (9)

Ariana Grande

My inspiration, no reason why,
Look at the smile on her face,
It would be a dream to stop and say hi,
She could take me to space,

Her songs are a hit,
It won't hurt a bit,
She's so legit,

Where could she be,
Finding my dream,
We could have tea,
We could be a team,

She's like a jewel,
Sparkling around,
But she's too cool,
I'm no fool.

Carla Maitena Burns (9)

My Magnificent Mum

My mum is my inspiration,
She influences my every action,
She expresses such compassion
And gives exceptional advice,
Which is always precise,
She is like a majestic gem,
That sparkles under the light,
This is a compelling sight.
She has no flaws,
Much to my applause,
She is one in a million,
I love you Mum...

Lola Terry-Corneille (13)

My Mum

My mum is here,
No need to fear,
I love her,
And she loves me too.

She is a retired writer,
Famous in India,
Her name etched in a book, but not on cotton,
Now these days have been forgotten.

Splish! Splash! Splosh!
Her cleaning just for me,
She is even kind to thee!
Remarkable she is.

Teghvir Singh (11)

I'll Be There

(For my sister, Sacha)

Don't worry, don't worry
I'll be there
Whenever you need me
I'll be there

You have been there for me
When I needed you
Whenever you need me
I'll be there

Now it is time for me to help
And do you need me?
Whenever you need me
I'll be there.

Don't worry!

Ruby Zelouf (6)

My Crazy Little Sister

My crazy little sister is so mad
She will never make me sad
Has tatty hair, she calls it 'swaggy'
Never leaves me alone, always nags me
Loves her L.O.L. dolls and toys
But hates 'smelly boys'
Runs away when I try to give her kisses
Can be a right little missus
I love you Ruby, I will always be your idol
And you will always be mine.

Lily Morris (10)

My Dad, My Hero!

My dad, my hero
I love you loads
You're my best friend ever
You'll always help with homework
You'll always help with making me better
Whenever I'm ever sad

Oh Dad, I love you to infinity and beyond
And don't forget the moon and back!

Just always remember
I love you!

Lily Doherty

Mummy And Daddy Are My Heroes

I like them very much.
They always take me on a bus ride and it's fun everywhere we go.
They always bring me presents for my birthday.
Mummy and Daddy always tell me news and stories.
Mummy and Daddy are very kind and funny.
I love them very much.
When I grow up I want to help others like Mummy and Daddy.

Nicole Abitimo (7)

My Idols

I see my mum,
Helping out in the kitchen late at night,
I see my dad,
Board games lost and won over and over again,
I see my brother,
Raucous laughter over something I can't quite remember,
I see my friends,
Never stop talking, never stop moving, never stop living,
I see my mirror,
Someone to stay with me for the rest of my life.

Megha Basu

My Best Brother

My best brother is the best
My best brother loves to rest.
My best brother loves the sun
My best brother likes to run.
My best brother loves cats
My best brother hates rats.
My best brother likes cuddles
My best brother likes bubbles.
My best brother likes dogs
My best brother hates frogs.

Elsie May Lightfoot (8)

Jane

I idolise Jane Austen,
I read her books very often,
From 'Pride and Prejudice' to 'Emma',
It has always been a pleasure.
She was truly a remarkable woman,
Let's just say I'm a big fan.
So next time you read one of her books,
Give her biography a look,
Then you will see why I idolise her.

Elise-May Jee (15)

Lord Of The Dance

L auren's legs landed her a role in the dance
A mazing opportunities await her at every chance
U p, up high on her pointy toes
R ealta School of Irish Dance is where her story started
E urope is where she sometimes goes
N ow you know nothing is impossible.

Ellyce Robinson

My Idol

Who is my idol,
Who might it be?
Here's a clue, they're very close to me

Who is my idol,
Who might it be?
They always laugh along with me

Who is my idol,
Who might it be?
They're always there looking out for me

Who is my idol,
Who might it be?
My big sister, Rose,
That's who I want to be.

Sasha Shadbolt (10)

My Uncle Eddie

If you knew my uncle Eddie,
You would know that he was always ready
To help with chores around the home,
He would even do them alone
But what do we do in this case
When we see him face-to-face?
We ask him has he done his chores
He says no because it bores!

Hannah Fallon

My Generous Mother

My mother is kind
and has shiny bright eyes
I love her dearly, there is no doubt in that
she is my heart and mind,
she always makes me feel warm
I kiss her with love and kindness,
oh, how she shines
she has a beautiful name
oh Sabahat, my dear mother,
do always be with me
and in my heart.

Maymuna Alma Ejaz Ahmed (9)

Who Do I Idolise?

A   n award-winning author,
N   othing which won't satisfy you,
T   he amazing novelist,
H   as written a great series of gripping stories,
O   bviously successful,
N   ever stopped entertaining me,
Y   ears of success with the second name Horowitz.

Tayyibah Begum (10)

Roald Dahl

Roald Dahl
Is never dull
He wrote great books
And was quite a good cook!
He discovered The Twits
And maybe Charlie had nits!
Fantastic Mr Fox
Couldn't fit BFG in a box!
James Henry Trotter
Rode on a giant peach
So his Aunt Sponge and Spiker
Were completely out of reach!

Jessica Dickens (10)

My Mami

You are amazing
You are the best

You are my favourite
You are my best friend

I love your hug
I love your care

I love you and kiss you
Because you love me too

I am so glad
I have you for a mother.

Ishma Ahmed (5)

My Idol

My idol is the best
Maybe better than the rest
When I'm down
She pulls me up
She is really funny
She's like the Easter bunny
Always giving out jokes
She teaches me to be nice
She is definitely full of sugar and spice
Her name is Mrs Rogers
My loving teacher.

Ayomide Deborah Aboyeji (10)

My Rad Dad

I idolise my dad,
Because he is quite rad,
My dad is never bad,
Thank god for that,
My dad is amazing at cricket,
Me and my dad never hit a wicket,
My dad loves me, no matter what,
I guess I hit the jackpot,
My dad is an extraordinaire and that's why I love him!

Imaan Siddique (12)

Mummy

My mummy's a chocolate sharer, hug machine and a best friend
She is always there for me,
Even though she works full time, she's always home for tea.
She buys me presents and makes me lovely food
My mummy is the best, she is amazing!

Isabelle Alice Williams

Parents

P eople watching over you,
A lways trying to make things better despite
R eally not knowing
E ach emotion that you feel.
N ights are full with love and care while
T rying to keep together their broken
S mile to save you.

Lucy Hollis (16)

Manchester City Is The Best Team Ever

Man City always wins the match
Their goalie has a great catch,
They tackle well,
All the way to the finish bell,
If they get a free kick,
You better be quick,
Oh how I want to be in their team,
It has always been my dream.

Jayden Fahy (6)

My Mum

M y marvellous mum
Y ou are always there for me

M aking me believe in myself and to always think of others
U nicorns and narwhals are our favourite things
M um, you make me want to try out new things.

Tess Diane Black (8)

My Hero

He is as strong as Thor,
Clever as Iron Man,
Braver than Captain America,
Crazy as the Hulk,
As fast as Flash,
Funny as Ant-Man,
Caring and sweet like Spider-Man,
He makes me feel magical like Doctor Strange's spells,
He is my superhero... My daddy!

Dhruv Bhudia (7)

Mum And Dad

My idols are really two people,
My mum and dad
Because I would love to be like them.
Find love and give love like them.
People say and I think that I look like my dad and act like my mum.
And that's quite true.
I love you, Mum and Dad.

Keeley Marie Seren Edwards

Mum

Sunshine beams out of my face whenever I see you,
You always brighten up my day, you make me chuckle too,
I want to tell you that you're ace and I love you so,
You make me smile inside my heart, I want you to know too.

Nadia Aber Okwera (10)

Mum

Roses are red, violets are blue,
All I want for my birthday is you.
When we need you,
You're right there,
With my big, snuggly, cuddly bear.
Dear Mum, you're the best,
You really do beat the rest!

Ruby Putnam (10)

A Cheeky Little Sister

A cheeky little sister being like a unicorn,
Sitting on the couch eating candy corn.
She plays and swims and also sings!
It looks like she has wings.
A cheeky little sister jumping on a trampoline,
Up in the sky like a queen!

Johanna Goron (8)

Doctor Who #13

I hate empty pockets,
I'm quite good with sockets,
Once played by Peter Capaldi,
Once played by a baldy,
I am a female Doctor,
So I sometimes wonder,
Does this change mean,
Equality?

Emaan Basharat (10)

Mum!

My mum is always there to save the day
She always knows what to say
She is the one who brought me to life
How tough I might be at times
She still loves me with all of her heart
And I love her too.

Libby Burbanks (9)

Wonder

So tender and sweet
Kindness flows like a rushing river
Spreading joy wherever you go.
You talk like an angel
So tender and sweet.
You are a beautiful star shining in the night.
You have beauty like a dazzling angel!

Afoma Anita Onwuokwu (10)

Malala

A girl
Standing, unafraid,
Against a sea of
Know your place.
But you are defiance
With hands to knead dough and fingers to
Turn the pages of a book.
You will look into the eyes of Death and say:
No.
No,
A hero.

Megan Angharad Lois Pritchard (16)

My Dad

I am so glad that you are my dad.
He always makes me smile, with him I never fail.
My dad is so strong, he can pick up a big rock.
My dad is the best dad ever
I love him forever.

Jasmin Pulkova

My Best Friend

She likes wearing horsey leggings
She likes watching Spirit
Her hair is brown and so is her eyes
We like to play together
She is my best friend in the whole wide world
She is my cousin Chloe.

Teddy Hawkins (6)

My Guardian

M agnificent
Y oung

G orgeous
U nique
A mazing
R espectful
D aring
I nspiring
A dventurous
N o one is as loving like you, Auntie.

Maryam Khanom (8)

My Mummy

My mummy is the lovely flower girl,
I give Mummy millions of kisses and hugs,
Mummy gets me lots of cars and takes me everywhere,
She is the best mummy in the world.

Noah Thomas Howard (5)

Sister

S   is for special
I   is for incredible
S   is for smashing
T   is for terrific
E   is for entertainment
R   is for respectful.

Maisy-Lou Tredinnick

My Daddy, Luke

My daddy works at Asda
My daddy tickles me to make me smile
I look up to my daddy because he is very, very kind
I love him because he is my daddy.

Sofia-Anne Cardall (6)

My Parents
A tanka

I love my parents,
They do lots of things with me,
They also love me,
They take me on holiday,
They are brilliant parents!

Freya Addison McKean (9)

My Mummy

Mummy is very friendly,
And she is very kind,
She is also very funny,
And gives us cake (sometimes).

Maya Devaskar (7)

Harry Bright

Harry Bright, beams like the night.
He studied the guitar in France,
He met Donna and asked her to dance,
Because she was his shining light.

She became his dancing queen,
If you know what I mean.
I'd love to marry Harry,
Or even just have one dance.
He is the light of my life.

We danced all night to Waterloo,
Where Napoleon did surrender.
Harry got locked out of his room,
He spoke French like 'va va voom!'
But all he could remember,
Was 'je suis locked out of de chambre'.

Clara Nelson (6)
Cheltenham College, Cheltenham

My Family

My family. Where to start?

My mummy is always bossy and silly
because she always forgets everything
and she snores really loud.

My sister, Amethyst,
is really good at doing her homework
and she is kind to me
but she does toxic farts.

My other sister, Krystal, is really lazy and mean to me
but sometimes we play together
and she is kind when she wants to be
but she does have stinky feet.

My little brother, Jensen, where to start?
I love him loads and he is very cute and cuddly
and sometimes he can be very naughty
but I still love him
and he's got really smelly feet.

That is everything about my family
which I will aways love.

Sapphire Balding (8)
Cooks Spinney Primary Academy & Nursery, Cooks Spinney

Untitled

My mummy is the best because I love her
She reads to me and sings to me
And we play make-believe together
She believes in everything I do
And tells me I can do anything when I grow up.

Gabriel Elms (8)
Cooks Spinney Primary Academy & Nursery, Cooks Spinney

My Amazing Family

My mummy, my mummy
She is sweet like honey
She'll love me forever
Even through stormy weather

My daddy, my daddy
He is oh, super handy
Just tell him your worry
He will fix it in a hurry

My brother, my brother
He is quite like no other
Even when he is annoying
He is still somewhat charming

My family, my family
This bond is for eternity
May we always live happily
And stay an amazing family.

Jachin Idehen-Nathaniel
Gorringe Park Primary School, Mitcham

My Incredible Sister

My incredible sister is definitely the best,
She always puts up with me, even though I'm a pest.

She is always inspiring me
And she spoils me with no fee.

She makes me happy when I feel sad
And not to mention, she never makes me feel bad.

Even though we argue, she is always there
And for me, she will always care.

My incredible sister is definitely the best,
She treats me so nice, it's as if I'm an important guest.

Lauryn Grace Wilkes (10)
Hazel Slade Primary Academy, Hazel Slade

The Special Person

My special person is nice in all ways
He is always kind, you should see his face
Every time he gets scared
When he snores, you know he is there
When he wakes, he is a pro
When I win, he pulls a face
Now his hair is going grey and he's getting old
He takes me to the park to play
He must be the best I've ever known
My special person has a lovely car
The special person saves me from the bad
His name is Dave and he's my dad...

Daniel Tonks (10)
Hazel Slade Primary Academy, Hazel Slade

Uncle Tim

U ncle Tim is really quite strong
N othing stops his arms from growing long
C atching a ball really is his thing
L aughing when I don't catch his fling
E verything that I do makes him laugh

T rying to make me follow in his path
I mages of him make me smile
M any times he has gone the extra mile.

Ezra Nathaniel Davies (9)
Hazel Slade Primary Academy, Hazel Slade

Love You, Grandad

My grandad gives me glee
When he sings songs to me
Sometimes happy or sad
It just makes me glad
He is the best grandad I ever had

My grandad is funny
When he tries to hop like a bunny
He gives me money
For being lovely

I love you, Grandad.

Noah Boden (9)
Hazel Slade Primary Academy, Hazel Slade

My Poetry Idol

My favourite person is David Walliams,
he is a famous child author.

His funny ideas make me laugh,
his ideas are as funny as a clown in a circus.

One of my favourite books that he wrote
is 'Gangsta Granny'.

He writes similes, alliteration
and many other interesting stuff.

I wish I could meet David Walliams
and ask him about the fabulous books he writes.

How does he get these ideas?
Where does it come from?
Who gives him the ideas?
Why does he write funny stories?

He is the best author ever,
I like his ideas all along his stories.
When his stories are there, I dig my mind to it.
I wonder if I can meet him one day.

Abdia Mohamed Irshad (8)
Kenmore Park Junior School, Kenton

Greatest Of All Time

Roger Federer is
Positively the greatest of all time
Without a doubt!

With an outstanding forehand
An unpredictable backhand
His smashing overhead is unretrievable
Without a doubt!

Sadly, his amazing career is nearly over
But he created a lifetime of memories
That we won't soon forget about
Without a doubt!

Without a doubt!
Win or lose, he wears a smile
Pats his opponent on the back
And never disrespects the referees - he's not like that

Without a doubt!
If he messes up on the easy shot
He never yells or makes a scene
Win or lose, his career has turned another page.

Without a doubt!
He is my idol
Not because of all his wins
Mostly because of his heart

Without a doubt!
Roger Federer is my idol
Strong, amazing and kind
Positively the greatest of all time
Without a doubt!

Melissa Beukes (9)
Lyford Cay International School, Bahamas

My Idol

She is old, but powerful
Strong, but weak
She is the reason I do what I love
I follow in her footsteps; one by one
I look up to her like a hawk
And for the future to come
I want to be just like her

Her career has ended
But mine has just began
And I could only hope to have the success she did
Because although
She is old, she is powerful
Strong, but weak
And for the future to come
I want to be just like her

She always did what she loved
Then something happened
Now her lovely daughter, Rosy
Lives to take care and to cherish her
This person that I love
Is the person that I follow
The person that I want to be

Even though she is old, she is powerful,
And even though she is strong, she is weak

And for the future to come
I want to be just like her
My dearest great grandmother.

Alexia Zatarain (9)
Lyford Cay International School, Bahamas

Tom Parr

Tom Parr. Hard house legend
Let's hope his music never ends.

I blast his beats
Even when I eat
I can't stop moving my feet
I can't even sleep, I play his tracks on repeat.

He makes me happy
I play him when I am sad.
His song, 'I Can't Help It'
Stops me feeling mad.

He inspired me to be
A DJ, you'll see!

He is the best DJ ever!
He is my man, my inspirational friend forever.

Jakey Brannigan
Marshfields School, Dogsthorpe

Randy Orton Is The Best

Randy Orton is the best
Better than all the rest!

He is the best wrestler in the world
His mighty power is out of control

Randy Orton does RKO
His music plays before every show

He pins wrestlers
And wins titles

Like the World Heavyweight Champion!

Randy Orton has nice hair
Randy Orton does not play fair

Randy Orton is the best
Better than all the rest!

James O'Doherty (14)
Marshfields School, Dogsthorpe

Have Some Fun Before You Die

Cristine, you make me laugh,
You even bathed in a red tea bath,
You love Starbucks and so do I,
But you prefer an almond milk chai.
Benny, Benny you're one of many,
You bring her tea but you know she has plenty,
Menchie, Zyler, Jenny too,
Holo, unicorn skin, the Pink Cow goes *moo!*
Polish Mountain was a blast,
But you didn't try to make it last,
Your coffin was stylish, chic and hollow,
You made it better by adding holo!
Before I go, I must say this one thing:
Never stop smiling and give it some bling.

Emma Louise Ross (14)
NCEA Duke's Secondary School, Ashington

Zlatan Ibrahimović

Z latan is a
L egendary football player. He
A chieved his
T alent from hard work, but not
A ll he does is good. He is a very
N aughty football player.

I nterestingly, a lot of football players are not as brave as him.
B ravery comes from saying things that are impossible, but in his
R eality, he can make them possible.
A nd he was a
H armful person
I n school, being known as one of the naughty students
M arvellously clever, when he was ten years
O ld, he told everybody that he would be a footballer and at the
V ery least, a billionaire. No one believed
I n him, but he
C ontinued to work until he reached the top.

Oxford Sixth Form College, Oxford

Ariana Grande

A riana Grande is a
R espectable and
I nteresting singer
A lso, she has a
N oteworthy
A bility to sing

G reat songs will
R emain forever in our hearts
A nd she could sing
N umerous
D itties
E loquently.

Luke Kim (17)
Oxford Sixth Form College, Oxford

Bob Ross

B ig, brown, bushy hair
O il painter master in my opinion
B eautiful paintings that I admire

R eally good tips on how to paint
O h, Bob Ross, you're that dude
S ketching and painting. Bob, you are so talented
S ketching and painting that I do too. I hope my art will be as good as yours too.

Hannah Potsworth (14)
Rosstulla School, Newtownabbey

Isco

I n my opinion, he is the best
S coring king
C entre back, thinking how to save
O h my, what a goal!

R unning down the pitch
E arning billions of pounds
A s fast as a runner
L earning football skills

M y player, I like Isco.

Ben Crawford (13)
Rosstulla School, Newtownabbey

Roblox

- **R** eally good for happiness
- **O** nline for all
- **B** locks and parts for all
- **L** ots of fun for all
- **O** nly for kids and teens
- **X** marks the spot for Roblox spot.

Lewis Donnelly (12)
Rosstulla School, Newtownabbey

Action

When I grow up I wish to be,
As famous, and as loved, as he.
Not only an actor, but a father too,
He's an inspiration for me and you.

"Everything is awesome", this wise man once said,
I think of his determination as I lie in bed.
The 'Lord Of Stars' he wanted to be called,
Cinema-goers around the world were amazed and enthralled.

If I ever met him, I would surely cry
I would give a big hug, and not want to say goodbye.
He's the alpha of a raptor pack and the father of them too,
You can text him on Insta, but he won't reply, he has many things to do.

He's every kid's hero, well mine anyway,
I would rather spend time with him than take £10,000 any day!
He's funny and a gentleman, what else is there to be?
I hope one day that he will be talking to me.

His name, you may ask, is Chris Pratt.
You can call him a man, but not a brat.
He is the one I look up to,
And now that you know my story, I hope you do too!

Finnley Higgins (11)
Southchurch High School, Southend-on-Sea

Why My Dad Inspires Me

My dad, he always leads me in the dark, he is my light in the dark,
He has always led me through things that help me, guide me and make me a better person,
He always cares about me and tells me if I haven't done something correct,
He will always help me through cold, dark emotions and times,
He will always be the dad everyone would want.
The countless times he has come and explained things for me to do
And things that would help me achieve my best in my school,
He would help me with my homework and not moan,
He would get me ready and not moan,
He wouldn't get annoyed if I did something wrong,
He would do things for me without a single fuss,
He helped me tie my first shoelace,
Congratulated me after the hundredth time,
He is my hero through any time,
He will be there in a matter of time,
Back when I was ten, he would always be there after school time,
Happy or sad,
I'm glad he will always be my dad.

Jacob Thomas Gawley (12)
Southchurch High School, Southend-on-Sea

The Person I Look Up To

Chris Pratt is a good actor,
He makes me laugh,
He makes me cry,
Especially when Yondu dies (Guardians of the Galaxy Vol 2)
Chris Pratt is a good actor.

Chris Pratt is very entertaining,
Especially in 'Guardians of the Galaxy',
He plays his role seriously,
Chris Pratt is very entertaining.

Chris Pratt is well known,
He has been in multiple films,
Comedy and drama films,
Chris Pratt is well known.

Chris Pratt is the main character in 'Guardians of the Galaxy'
He was also a leader of a raptor pack (Jurassic World)
He played his character excellently
Chris Pratt is the main character in 'Guardians of the Galaxy'.

Chris Pratt was in 'Jurassic World',
He fought an indominus rex,
And dashed through a jungle with a pack of raptors,
He was also the father of the pack of raptors,
Chris Pratt was in 'Jurassic World'.

Gaius Ware (12)
Southchurch High School, Southend-on-Sea

Adam Peaty

While you're on your way to school,
He is already doing drills in the pool,
When you're getting ready to go home,
He is lifting weights to help get toned.

He swims seven miles a day,
Dreaming of bettering himself in his own way,
He breaks his own records,
His best is under 26 seconds.

He does not care about medals,
But does not like to come in second,
He inspires thousands around the globe,
And I am just one of those.

He gives one hundred percent,
In every single swimming event,
He wants to always be the best,
At swimming sprints on his breast.

He has reached his ambition,
To inspire the next generation,
In interviews he can be very cheeky,
He is the legend, Adam Peaty.

Arrianne Lea (12)
Southchurch High School, Southend-on-Sea

My Mum

You make my world so bright,
You are my shining light,
When I cry,
I'd have to lie,
You've always been by my side,
Even when I was shy.

You rocked my cot,
Even when I was hot,
When I do a test,
You know I tried my best,
You are the best person ever,
And I know you would leave me never.

You have always been there for me,
All the things you buy me,
You made me the person I am today,
With you, I wouldn't regret any day,
When I struggled,
We cuddled,
Whenever I'm sick,
You help me get fixed.

You are my best friend,
A bond that will never end!

Jaimie Parks (12)
Southchurch High School, Southend-on-Sea

I Love You

You are my days and nights,
You are my shining lights.
You are my angel,
You rocked my cradle.

You are always kind to me,
My guardians, always there for me.
You are always by my side,
Even when I want to cry.
Whenever we are sick,
We help each other get fixed.
Whenever we struggled,
We always cuddled.

You are my stars so bright,
You taught me how to write.
Although I was weak,
You taught me how to speak.

You are the ones who raised me up.
You are the ones who backed me up.
You don't even have a clue,
How much I love you,
Mama and Nana, I love you so much.

Ana-Albina Vreme (12)
Southchurch High School, Southend-on-Sea

Mum

Have you ever heard the saying 'I don't have eyes in the back of my head'?
Because my mum uses it all the time,
Especially when I'm fighting with my brother,
She used to tuck me into bed,
And puff my pillow and pull up my cover.

Last week, I was rehearsing a play,
She always knows what to say,
To make me feel better when I'm glum,
She helps me with my homework, because I'm dumb.

When she was younger,
She worked hard at school,
(At least that's what she says!)
She still works hard now and does not get to rest.

I love my mum,
Thanks for what you've done.

Madeline Atkin (12)
Southchurch High School, Southend-on-Sea

Dear Grandfather

Little sunflower,
Come look at me,
I am your soldier, your friend,
Please see,
That though you are gone,
My heart doesn't feel,
You disappeared,
And left me ill,
On that cold night,
While full of shivers,
You were by my side,
Holding your gifts to me,
One was love, the other respect,
But still I wonder...
Why have you left?
You were always so funny,
Kept calling me a bunny,
As well as that drawing,
I still remember you snoring.
It's harsh, but I got to get by,
But I'll always look at you in the sky.

Khadija Nobre Dos Santos Costa (12)
Southchurch High School, Southend-on-Sea

Mum

Mum, she's brought me on the Earth, so I need to carry on her path,
She never lets me down and always makes sure everyone is happy but herself.
She makes me smile on a rainy day and makes sure I never have a frown on my face.
My life wouldn't be the same without this amazing woman with me every day,
My music performances, my athletics, she's never let me down,
Always on the side track to cheer me on.
She's there for me when I'm alone and there for me when I'm not,
In hospital, at home or at school, she's always ran around for me.

Chloe Downs (11)
Southchurch High School, Southend-on-Sea

I Want To Be Like My Mum

She helps me with things,
She tells me what to do,
She looks after my sisters,
And looks after me too.

She is the best!
The one I can trust,
We revise for my tests,
Which I know I must.

I have to help with the dishes,
I do not blame her,
For I have two sisters,
Two natural disasters.

I want to be like her,
She gets it all done,
No matter the hour,
And she is very fun!

She is my idol,
And for years to come,
Even when I was very little,
I love my mum.

Molly Phillips (12)
Southchurch High School, Southend-on-Sea

Dad

Dad, you may smell and you may be a pain
But when I need a light to guide me
Or when I feel afraid
You are there to build me up
You are my flashlight
You are my hero, you are my helpline
You are my dad
You support me in my goals
You show me the way, you light me up
You build my confidence every day
I will appreciate you
Because you make me stronger
You are making me a man
Making memories to share forever
You cheer me on, through good and bad
I am glad you're my dad.

Alfie Hunt (12)
Southchurch High School, Southend-on-Sea

Mum

The person I love the most
I love her dearly from head to toe
She means the world to me
And I love her a load

She's always there for me
When I'm feeling down
To clear the clouds
From a sunny side

My life wouldn't be worth living if I didn't have her
There by my side
To guide me through life
When I have no one else

She swoops in and saves the day
Like a superhero would do
I will always be there for her
No matter what we go through.

Jessica Poole (12)
Southchurch High School, Southend-on-Sea

Mum

I love you, Mum
Through thick and thin
I love you, Mum
With my whole heart

Dear Mum
I admire you
I cannot explain how supportive you are
You have worked hard
You will always work hard
And I want to be just like you

I want to have three kids, like you
I want to be independent, like you
I want to be the world's best mother in the world
But that spot is taken
Taken by you

I love you, Mum
I admire you, Mum
I want to be like you.

Emily Potts (12)
Southchurch High School, Southend-on-Sea

My Uncle

When I grow up, I want to be like my uncle
Successful, kind and generous
A boy in blue
No particular hue

Fights crime
In a matter of time
He is my hero
Although he looks a bit like an armadillo

A police officer
He will run a kilometre
I don't want to be split up with him
Even though I can't go into the gym
A man in blue
Will always pull through
Never feels ill
Has a brain filled of skill.

Joe Davies (12)
Southchurch High School, Southend-on-Sea

My Mum

My mum makes me smile,
Makes me happy,
Makes me worth my while.

She gives me ideas,
Sometimes she's in tears,
But when she's not,
She laughs a lot.

My mum makes me smile,
Makes me happy,
Makes me worth my while.

She is never boring,
Even when it's pouring,
And she doesn't like snoring,
But when she sleeps,
She cannot wait to get up in the morning.

Alex Taylor (12)
Southchurch High School, Southend-on-Sea

My Idol

My brother, my idol
My hero, who never gives up
He inspires me
And my friends and family

Determined, resilient and persevered to
A great sportsman
A team player on the pitch
In games he loves a glitch

As I look up to him
He'll always help me
I know he's got my back
And he shares his Tic Tacs

I wish I could be just a little bit like him.

Thomas Morgan Hucker (12)
Southchurch High School, Southend-on-Sea

My Dad

My dad is an amazing person
He works so hard; it makes me smile
And all the treats I get
The amount of effort he puts in
Inspires me so much
He means the world to me

The way he balances family and work
Is truly inspirational
The lessons he has taught me, will remain in my brain
I am extremely grateful for this

When I grow up, I would love to be like him.

Will Turner (11)
Southchurch High School, Southend-on-Sea

My Dad

My dad may not be the smartest
But he is the big-heartedest
He's always there to have fun
Even when there is no sun

He is the light that guides me through
He even knows kung fu
He is a guardian
He protects me all the time

When I see him, I look and think
I truly have the best dad there can be
I sometimes believe
My dad is God (old and wise).

Alfie Peck (12)
Southchurch High School, Southend-on-Sea

Mum

You are the best,
You really need a rest,
From all your three children.

Although we may be naughty,
And think that we are haughty,
We still love you,
For all the things you do.

You are very funny,
And make my day feel sunny.
You are caring,
And daring,
Forgiving,
Understanding and loving.

That is why I call you Mum.

Erica Bristow (12)
Southchurch High School, Southend-on-Sea

My Mum Inspires Me

My mum is the best
She fills me with glee
My mum, the nicest to me, that's her
If you don't know that, then duh!
My mum really inspires me
She knows that I've got talent
And if she ever goes
I will miss her
Now this is the last verse
Which my mum made me rehearse
I love my mum
Lastly, she inspires me
Because she's my family.

Dylan Jewell (12)
Southchurch High School, Southend-on-Sea

I Admire My Mum Because...

I love my mum
She is not dumb
When I get hurt
She calls me by my name, Burt
My mum inspires me
Because she used to help me change my nappy
So I'd be happy
But if I was naughty
She would give me a slappy
I love my mum
Because she is not dumb.

Bobby Reynolds (12)
Southchurch High School, Southend-on-Sea

My Author Idols

I idolise John McCrae,
Who fought in wars day to day,
He wrote the poem 'In Flanders Fields'
Which makes me remember
Those poor souls
Who stood strong to be our shield.

I idolise Roald Dahl,
Even though he died,
Which made me cry.
He tried and tried,
To gets lots of poems done,
But unfortunately, he has only written one.

I idolise many other poets,
That you too probably know,
Even though,
They lived a long time ago.

One day I would like to be an idol,
A young writer like myself,
Looking up at my work,
Standing proud on the shelf.

Alexander Guérin-Hassett (9)
Wouldham All Saints CE Primary School, Wouldham

Young Writers Information

We hope you have enjoyed reading this book – and that you will continue to in the coming years.

If you're a young writer who enjoys reading and creative writing, or the parent of an enthusiastic poet or story writer, do visit our website **www.youngwriters.co.uk**. Here you will find free competitions, workshops and games, as well as recommended reads, a poetry glossary and our blog. There's lots to keep budding writers motivated to write!

If you would like to order further copies of this book, or any of our other titles, then please give us a call or order via your online account.

Young Writers
Remus House
Coltsfoot Drive
Peterborough
PE2 9BF
(01733) 890066
info@youngwriters.co.uk

Join in the conversation!
Tips, news, giveaways and much more!

YoungWritersUK   @YoungWritersCW